The Profitable Architect

The Profitable Architect

How to attract new projects and work with clients that understand the value of good design

CHRISTIAN HOGUE
ARCHITECT PROFITS, INC.

Published by Advantage, Charleston, South Carolina.
Member of Advantage Media Group.

Printed in the United States of America.

ISBN: 978-1-59932-200-1
LCCN: 2010924133

DISCLAIMER

This book is designed to provide information about the subject matter covered. It is sold with the understanding that the publisher and author are not hereby engaged in rendering legal, psychological, or other professional services. If expert assistance is required, the services of a competent professional should be sought.

The author is available for consultation on a professional basis.

Every effort has been made to make this book as complete and accurate as possible, but in the event of any mistakes in typography or content, this text should be used only as a general guide.

The purpose of this book is to educate and entertain. The author and publisher shall have neither liability nor responsibility to any person or entity with respect to any loss or damage caused or alleged to be caused directly or indirectly by the information contained herein.

TABLE OF CONTENTS

Foreword

By Jeff Rice

"The more I want to get something one, the less I call it work."
Richard Bach

Ten years ago, my partner and I recognized a severe need for education resources for the architectural and design community. With the constant flux of new technologies, codes and products, these professionals needed educational tools available to *ALL* design professionals.

From this notion, we created **AEC Daily**, a Web-based learning center geared toward the design industry providing 24-hour access to building product information, industry news, educational opportunities, discussion forums, and much more.

When Christian Hogue presented to me the idea of creating a continuing education course on marketing for architects,

I was extremely excited about the idea and proud that he asked me to help create it.

Christian's intimate knowledge of the trials that architects face was immediately clear when we collaborated the course. The topic of marketing *for* architects was long overdue. ***AEC Daily*** has been in business nearly ten years; we host a library of over 250 courses, yet Christian is the ONLY individual to present this topic. This book, like his course, is insightful, empathetic, and challenges architects to incorporate new tools to which they are not accustomed.

With our current economy, more and more architects are working solo or in smaller firms. Yes, the business is out there for you – but the skills to capture and keep clients needs to be more and more refined. That is why this book is critical for any design professional seeking to find and grow business.

Christian, who started his first project in a small firm in St. Louis over twelve years ago, has a unique point of view for a person teaching about marketing (and telling us why we're on the verge of insanity!). He will teach you a systematic way to get results, how to avoid common pitfalls, and express your own unique abilities and effectively market them.

The result we all want for our business is to have a consistent flow of new clients who understand the value of good design and good product. This book provides you a road map to develop these clients faster and with fewer mistakes.

It's about time someone teaches architects that every person in the office is really part of a sales team, starting with the person answering the phone.

Way to go, Mr. Hogue!

Jeff Rice

President, AEC Daily Corp.

www.aecdaily.com

A Few Words Before We Begin

"When you reach for the stars, you may not quite get one, but you won't come up with a handful of mud either."

Leo Burnett

Recently, one of my social acquaintances was talking about the popular cable TV show *Mad Men*, set in the "golden age of advertising."

Why was it a golden age? Some of the greatest men ever involved with business promotion lived and worked at the same time, with their lives overlapping. Concepts and strategies of Ogilvy, Reeves, Caples, Hopkins, Burnett and other icons underlie critical points in my programs for architects to find specific clients and to sell their services.

I would like to claim to be the inventor of the strategies we will cover in this book, but I simply stand on the shoulders of these giants to amalgamate what they have showed will work so you can use those ideas with good results.

WHAT? ISN'T NOW THE GOLDEN AGE FOR ADVERTISING?

Mad Men cannot address the huge shift that advertising and marketing at large took in the 1970s and '80s – a shift that broke from the foundation based on the research of the greats. Until then, the most worthy promotion motto was, "We sell. Or else." The newer philosophy was, "We'll make it look pretty and creative, and perhaps you'll sell something. Good luck."

That breaking of the foundation of good advertising is what led to the lousy and unmeasurable results that most marketing delivers today. When is the last time you've heard of an award given to an agency that produced the best sales results, be it for an actual product or a service? Never. It's always about which ad in a magazine looks the best, and it's the same for any other medium.

About the same time that change occurred, many professionals, including architects, started to actively promote their services. They looked to the ad industry for guidance and immediately began to use what *doesn't* work. That would be like an architect consulting with a Third World street worker about energy and building codes needed to improve an old edifice.

How does this translate to you, the architect firm owner? For much of the 20th century, architects were forbidden from marketing their services. They weren't allowed to advertise in any way except for a line or a business card in the Yellow Pages. Anything beyond that would bring censure from professional associations. One might wonder what they were trying to protect. Even when the associations relaxed these rules in the 1970s, architects were still slow to create and implement marketing tools for their firms.

However, the 1980 recession saw the beginning of an interest and a need in architectural marketing. Architects had to put aside age-old prejudices and start blowing their own horns. Unfortunately, they started doing so after the shift in advertising.

Soon after, the Internet became a powerful tool that allowed even the smallest firms to look like multinational ones. In some ways, the Internet leveled the playing field because of low cost and long reach. But that was back then: Now, using the Net for marketing has mostly downsides since most firms use it the same way.

That "sameness" essentially erases any benefits since the same information too often is provided in the same format. What's left is the contact information for the prospect visiting the website of an architect.

Today, architects spend on average between 5 to 7.5 percent of their expenses on marketing while mostly competing for the same clients and projects in the same way. The expected results (new projects) are difficult to obtain, since the clients are facing the same things from most architects. As opposed to competing for the same projects, architects would benefit from investing their time, energy and money in search of unique clients with the perfect projects.

Why do today's architects feel a shame at exposing their names as a form of promotion? Most architects want to make the world a better place without attracting too much attention to themselves. A few "star-chitects" play loud and hard but often are harshly criticized by peers.

When looking back at what your peers once did, you might wonder what went so wrong. The image below illustrates how architects once marketed themselves. That day is long gone, This image below of what architects used to do to "market" themselves is long gone and it is hard to think that it could come back.

Yes, we still know who designed this building!

How can architects expect to make the world a better place when most compete for the same projects for the same clients? Just a small fraction of the population will ever contact an architect to work on an actual project. Would it make more sense to open your doors to more people, especially those who would not otherwise think of working with an architect? I believe so, and this book will explore how you can do this and have a profitable practice.

DID I SAY "PROFITABLE"?

Yes! This book will explore strategies and tools that you should put in place in your own practice to be profitable as a first goal. I insist that without profits, an architect cannot enjoy, benefit and keep his practice, and therefore cannot produce the highest level of architecture. The second one cannot go without the first one.

The September 2009 issue of the Architects magazine included a successful article on successful practices. One aspect in determining which practices were most successful was their profitability. The magazine felt the need to state this: "A cynic might say that, by scoring firms based in part on profitability (i.e. revenue per number of employees), we reward scrooges who run their offices like sweatshops."

I praise the magazine for not being afraid to use this tool to measure the success of a firm. Why is it a bad thing for architects to think they deserve financial success while producing the highest level of architecture?

No wonder most architects can't get and don't even ask for decent fees. They don't believe they deserve them. If you believe you deserve decent fees for the quality of the services you are providing, then this book is for you. If you don't believe that architects deserve decent fees, stop reading now.

Let's think about this for a minute. An architect who cannot make enough profit to take time off, for example, won't be able to explore and find new ideas and concepts to share with future clients. Without enough profit to take time off, the architect won't get the rest and replenishment to bring new and better projects to clients. Not a good outcome for either architect or client.

In this book I will share methods and strategies that will bring you and your practice more clients, more projects, and more profits than you currently think possible.

Christian Hogue

Christian Hogue

CEO, Architect Profits, Inc.

INTRODUCTION

"Fools say experience is the best teacher.
I prefer to learn from other people's experiences."
Otto von Bismarck

WHO AM I, AND WHY WOULD YOU LISTEN TO ME?

Let me answer this question.

In more than ten years in the industry, I've been fortunate to have worked on a wide range of successful projects, with a variety of experiences.

My first project, working in a five-person office, was on a suburban house remodel in St. Louis. All drawings were done by hand, the good old-fashioned way, and I loved it. After that, I worked on many retail tenant improvements to a big parking structure. Imagine how many discussions I had with the structural engineer wanting to do a nice square box – not exactly what I had in mind. That led me to various firms working on diverse projects in the United States and as far as Asia.

Several years ago, I decided that it was time toto start working on my own and to stop working for others, for peanuts. I'm sure you know what I mean by that. It was time to take a big career step and start working on my own projects. I quickly realized what that actually meant was working on clients' projects – and what I needed to do was find those clients. But how?!?

I wanted to start the right way and no longer be underpaid for my services. I knew that what I had seen in the different firms I worked for was not the way I wanted to run my business. I purchased and read all books I could find on marketing for architects, and I was quickly disappointed.

Why? Most information was very general – how big firms can please clients, not how someone like me could get the right clients who would pay fairly and appreciate good design.

My next step was to ask architects with smaller firms what was working for them. I even did surveys. Most of them were doing the same thing: hoping to get clients via networking wherever and whenever they could. They were all complaining about the same lack of results. (And this was even before recessionary times.)

NO ONE SEEMED TO KNOW WHAT TO DO.

Learning early on that success in architecture requires more than project expertise, I looked at what worked for other professionals in other industries. How did they promote their services at the price they deserved? Something really far from what we were told in architectural school.

When I was 18, long before I knew I'd want to go into graduate school for architecture, I worked at a design store in Montreal, Canada. The manager decided to hold a contest for employees: Who could sell the most on a daily basis while she was on vacation? The store's philosophy was to greet customers within two minutes and tell them about weekly specials. The sales staff had to bug everyone.

I won the contest, far ahead of my coworkers. The CEO of the Canadian division of this U.S company actually called me to ask about my sales strategies. I'm very direct and just told him what I did: "I don't talk to the people who look at the little knick-knacks. I just talk to those who are looking at the biggest pieces of furniture."

He told me, of course, that I had to talk to everyone. If I did that, I responded, I would not have enough time with the serious buyers, and I pointed to my results to show I was right. Nonetheless, my manager told me to stop what I was doing. It was against policy.

I've always tried to think outside my box, looking for better ways to get results even if I had to break others' rules. And what I finally found through my research was grand: You can get measurable results from your marketing efforts.

I knew I had to share this. There are simple ways to find out what works. There are concrete rules and strategies that apply to any professional selling services, and they work time and time again. Instead of just hoping for the best, you need a well-defined system with steps that get proven results. You can get the business you want, and there is room for all architects willing to do what it takes.

I created the Elite Architects Programs, which include a step-by-step system that architects willing to work on their practice, as opposed to only in their practice, can easily use to finally get the results they've been striving for. The different levels of the Elite Architects Programs are all fully guaranteed, and I have great member feedback, from the United States and from other countries.

In this book, I wanted to give more architects easier access to information about strategies and systems I have put together over the years. I can guarantee you that your business will change for the better by reading it. Most of those rules are really simple; the only problem is that you need to know what they are so you can apply them.

Here is one example of a marketing mistake done over and over again: It's not enough to do some networking. If you don't systematically follow up with people who get in touch with you through your website or in person, you will lose them. There are some straightforward and effective ways to do this, but it needs to be done the right way and in the right order.

Many architects claim to be doing what they really want in their practices. But most of the time they are stuck with clients and projects they don't want, but which they need to pay the bills. The problem often is they don't understand crucial marketing concepts and how to get a prospect to accept a project and service that can be expensive.

The vast majority of such projects are not referred, but are attracted to practices by *direct-to-consumer marketing.* That's the sort of marketing that most architects just don't understand – and that's good, since it puts you in the category of #1 when you do use those strategies.

Was my thinking always like this? Of course not. It was a long road, with plenty of mistakes. Despite my mistakes, I was able to gradually build a system solely via the use of external marketing. First, I systematized different marketing strategies and tools and developed my sales system. (Yes, even architects must have a sales system.) Then I packaged everything up to ensure that architects could apply information and attract more of the projects and clients they want.

The tools and strategies that I will share will help you get clients who understand the value of good design and appreciate the services of an architect.

WHO SHOULD READ THIS BOOK

Let me be clear here: This book is really meant for solo architects and for firms of up to ten employees, or roughly 80 percent of U.S. firms. Can others read this book and find valuable information? Absolutely, especially young architects thinking of starting a practice. Firm owners with more than ten employees will also find important strategies.

Three types of architects will benefit from this book. The first are those with years of experience and extensive but underutilized training and skills. The second are mid-career, looking for change, better results, and a new adventure. The third type are those new to the profession who want to skip others' mistakes and simply find and apply what works as they develop their practices.

A critical aspect of this book is that it proposes strategies to promote architectural services so more people benefit from them. Let's take for granted here that architectural services improve people's lives in general, regardless of the aesthetic aspects of each project.

This book also will show you that it is possible to ask for and receive the fees that any professional providing services of the highest quality deserves. Too many architects get lower fees than they want, complain, but don't know what to do about it. We used to joke about this future reality while I was in grad school: "You need to have passion in this profession, because you won't make a dime for it."

Fox News interviewed a celebrity hair stylist in Manhattan, Ted Gibson, who charges $950 for an hour to an hour and a half of service, coloring, pampering, etc. He also charges a 20 percent tip. "What do you get for that $950?" Gibson was asked. His response: "You get ME!" His strategy for making money seems to be more than pure luck: He has several clips on YouTube offering free advice, and he sends a weekly newsletter.

Two concepts here are very important to understand, though most architects would consider them crazy:

1. This is a prime example of extreme flexibility in pricing when the right "set-up" is in place to allow it.

2. This savvy stylist understands that people are buying who he is, not what he does.

The hairstylist example is a reminder that your fees should be what you think you deserve, not what you think people are willing to give you. If you have the right systems in place, clients will accept your fees.

If you don't believe it is possible to use new strategies to quickly have a successful practice, go right now to page 218 and read Tim's story. It will assure you that what follows in this book is possible. You will know you can have a successful practice in any type of economy with the right tools and a system in place. It is critical that you read that success story now so you can open your mind and be receptive. Otherwise, chances are you will not pay attention to what you are reading nor act on it.

IN THIS BOOK...

This book will focus on the residential work done by smaller firms, especially those with ten or fewer people. However, all strategies and tools reviewed here do apply to other building types: same strategies, just different words.

The first part of this book covers what you should do differently to improve results when prospects contact you. Two specific tools will provide you with critical information you can use right now. One is your website. The other is an undervalued piece of office equipment: your phone.

In the second part, you will learn what to put in place to work with people who had not been considering an architect. You will gain projects without fighting with your peers, and you will do so by positioning yourself as their only emotional and logical choice. I will show you exactly what type of external marketing you need – effective strategies and tools to attract clients who weren't looking to work with you.

You will also learn critical systems to use once you have attracted those prospects. These include screening to determine who will say "yes," and a specific sales system to increase your project acceptance rate.

The third section includes real-life success stories. Besides Tim, other examples are people I've contacted and who are not part of my Elite Architect Programs. I want to show you successful practices and what is happening out there. It's quite an eye-opener.

In this book I will *not* talk about the following as "marketing strategies":

- **Passion:** If you don't have passion for your work, you should not be in this profession.

- **Authenticity:** If you don't have authenticity, you are in the wrong profession.
- **"Word of mouth":** Don't expect your prospect to do the leg work for you. Do it yourself, and you'll get much better results.
- **Experience:** Architects with experience will be better at persuading prospects to work with only them, but good strategies should apply to all architects, not just those already getting the work.
- **Reasonable fees "for the client":** If it's not reasonable for you, you should not work on that project.

As you read, you'll find concepts that change your thinking. You'll be closer to getting more of what you want and deserve out of your practice. I'll push some of your buttons to get you moving, so fasten your seat belt and enjoy the ride.

PART I

The Basics...

CHAPTER 1

The Next Golden Age Has Arrived

"Too many architects with advanced skills are 'all dressed up' with no clients to work with… and those skills go to waste."

Christian Hogue

You now find yourselves in the biggest golden age in architecture EVER, with the ultimate in construction speed, advanced programs to produce the documents for the most complex buildings, and the best materials available out there. With the right project acceptance strategies and tools, you now have better access and better reach to the type of clients and projects you want, in your own region and virtually anywhere in the world.

Never before in the history of architecture has there been such expertise. Every practitioner can have access to virtually any type of project they wish. In the last 15 years, the number of specialized courses and software has surpassed anything previously available in institutions of higher learning.

Combine the advances in technology and speed with the availability of higher education (think of being LEED accredited, the expansion of BIM, rendering programs, etc.), and there has never been a better time to practice architecture.

You can ignore this golden age and choose not to participate in the party, or you can reap the huge financial and professional rewards that you deserve. Which is it going to be?

A large group of architects are ready for the party. They are specialists who have kept up with technology, and generalists who have taken vast amounts of advanced training.

However, this is the equivalent of being all dressed up and having no place to go (except, in architectural terms, we'll say "all dressed up and no projects to go to"). Most in this group have some false thinking about what gets you to the party. We'll deal more with that in Chapter 4.

Hopefully, even if you are still gaining the skills you want, you will join the party. That way you can give the clients who really need you the services they expect – and isn't that what this is really all about?

There's a prerequisite for the party, besides knowledge of your profession. To apply that knowledge, you must have access to a rarefied level of specialized business and marketing knowledge to be able to attract the projects you want. Most architects will never be willing to acquire what it takes to join the fun. Most just won't go to the effort, or invest the necessary time and money. Some even will pretend it is not for them or does not exist. On the other hand…

If you are serious about joining the party, this book will give you the keys to open the door and get you inside to that punch bowl. I guarantee it.

WHAT YOU NEED TO KNOW ABOUT TODAY'S NEW ARCHITECTURAL ECONOMY

I know what you are thinking: The current economy is in the tank, so why should I bother with project acceptance strategies, systems, training, or even thinking about the future? Answer: because the architectural economy is undergoing a radical shift, and you need to be ready for it.

That's why a systematic and repeatable project acceptance system is a "must-have" for any architect who wants to survive and prosper during this recession and also wants to thrive, with real profit, once the new architectural economy is fully engaged.

The good old days when the phone rang to announce a new project on a silver platter will not come back. People don't expect the same as before and don't search for what they want as they used to. You need to be ready for this new reality.

Systems are ways for you to save time, energy, money and stress. Few architects have been trained to put any kind of a project acceptance (or sales) system into place, and so they too often ad-lib each time, making the same mistakes over and over.

Without a reliable system, you probably don't have a clue why some clients used to surprise you by calling your office and going forward with a project. Somehow, you just got lucky, though many of your peers were equally capable. By now, you are certainly aware that to depend on luck to get a new project is no longer an option, even more so with the changes at hand.

Most architectural firms cannot currently adjust their attitude, their creativity, their pursuit of new clients, and their focus on how to create more value to their clients to be sure they are not just a commodity. That used to be fine, but no longer.

In today's new economy, the business owner, including the architectural business owner, has three options that will either lead to failure, stagnation, or great success over the next several years for his or her practice.

The first option is "survivor" mode: They can just try to subsist in the current economic downturn and hope for the best. This is a tough option since it puts a great deal of pressure on the team and the owner. Usually those who choose this option think they have to lower their fees to get new clients. Worst case scenario is that they are willing to take new projects, any projects, even knowing they won't make any profit on the job. For some strange reason they hope that by doing the same as before, things will stay as before. Not a smart strategy.

The second one is the "no-future" strategy. Those who go with this option are cutting down on fees, employees, their ambitions and activities. One of the first expenses they cut is for their marketing. The results speak for themselves: This is not working well for those firms. Usually they complain all the time about everything, especially their clients. It's never their fault if things are not as they would like them to be.

The third option is to learn new ways to get the type of practice they want, especially in this new economic reality. The best way to achieve this is to continually investigate new forms of value creation in every aspect of their practices. The most successful architects are the ones doing two things. First, they are taking advantage of any innovations in technology by learning how these advances can help them successfully promote their practice. Second, they are making sure that they stay away from being a commodity for their existing and potential clients.

What you need to understand is that with this new architectural economy, you can do very well financially and help more clients than you thought possible – if you have both the architectural and non-architectural skills to make it happen. The processes and strategies that follow are already changing architects' lives. If the concepts can help them, they'll help you too.

I'm sure that we both agree that in this new economy, architectural skills are a must. Now it's time that we both agree that non-architectural skills are equally as important. You will shortly find some success strategies never before revealed outside my Elite Architect Programs to get access to those skills. But first, let's take a closer look at the type of clients you can expect to find out there.

CHAPTER 2

Who Are these Clients?

"Your clients decide to invest in themselves through you."
Christian Hogue

There are three types of clients that you should expect to find in the marketplace. At present, you may think a client either wants to work with an architect or must, or else doesn't want to and doesn't have to. But read on. It is critical that you have a clear understanding of what you are dealing with to ensure better results.

CLIENT TYPE #1

The first type of client constitutes the majority of the population. This client truly does not have the money to pay for a new project done by an architect and will very likely never have the money. In a utopian world, architects would serve them all – but mankind thus far has failed miserably to create Utopia, and I don't want to try any new versions!

This is the group that most architects blame when they "complain and moan" about why they can't seem to put their skills to work. They say, "People don't understand the value of architecture and just can't afford this." *However, the real issue is a failure in their own systems whereby the clients who really can't afford working with an architect don't remove themselves from the screening process.* With the right screening tools as part of your marketing and project acceptance system, these clients won't eat up any of your valuable time. They quickly select themselves out.

CLIENT TYPE #2

This is the small percent of the population who not only have serious architectural problems or dreams, but also have the money to deal with them.

In fact, some have *far more money* than required to get the best project for their needs. The real issue is that they don't have the money *for you*. They'll gladly tell you cost isn't a concern, yet decide that the benefit they'll gain from working with an architect isn't big enough to warrant giving that money to you.

These clients have discretionary cash, but for them architecture is simply not a high priority. (When it comes to cars, they are often not afraid to spend more than $100,000 for a toy that will last only a few years with no resale value.)

Indeed, some have millions in the bank, but it is just not their priority to go through the process of working with an architect to get a project that would suit them. This is a reality for residential architecture, and any other type of architecture for that matter, no matter how much you pester the client. Because they could afford even the most expensive options, these people are probably the most frustrating to deal with: They can jump through all the screening hoops you put into place to eliminate the low-cost "tire-kickers." Their attitude is: "Why deal with an architect when you can get something already done for you?"

Those first two types will lose you too much time, energy and money. It is better to focus on getting the type of clients who will say "yes." That way, you will get more new projects while keeping your sanity.

CLIENT TYPE #3

Okay, that takes care of the two types of clients that you DON'T want to spend much of your time with. Finally, the client you love: the one who has the money and is willing to pay for the services of an architect. This client understands the value of good design and the benefits of working with you. Sometimes, this type of client lives modestly and doesn't appear to be rich. If you've read *The Millionaire Next Door* by T. Stanley and W. Danko, you'll find many of their characteristics explained.

In this book, we will cover not only how to land a client who is looking to work with an architect, but also a client who isn't even thinking of working with one.

You will see that there are huge benefits in starting to think outside your architect's hat when it comes to whom you should and can work with. Why fight with all your peers for the obvious prospects when you can get better benefits from the ones who are hiding, while helping a larger section of the world around you?

Now that we have looked at client types, let's shift our attention to the three biggest architectural insanities of many of your peers. (But not you, of course…)

CHAPTER 3
Architectural Insanity

"Insanity: doing the same thing over and over again and expecting different results."
Albert Einstein

Architect, for some reason your thinking can sometimes get out of whack via the educational process. In general, we are led to believe in architectural school that if we are nice and if we have strong architectural skills, clients will come to us. It is obviously no longer the case in today's new architectural economy.

I'm sure that you are well aware that for some reason, some firms are thriving in today's economy and some other firms are struggling to keep their doors open, even though they have produced great work and even have won awards. But still, the projects are just no longer coming in.

Let's take a closer look at the three biggest insanities done over and over again by too many of your peers that prevent them from attracting new projects., so you can avoid them.

ARCHITECTURAL INSANITY #1:

THE ATTEMPT TO BE ALL THINGS TO ALL PEOPLE

Too often, architects are very old thinkers in the way they approach their marketing, if they do any marketing at all. Most marketing has remained unchanged and relatively primitive for a long time. The result is that too often, when a practice does promote its services, it starts to feel the strain and the frustration of marketing that no longer works without knowing what is actually not working.

We've talked about it: "Fighting" the same competition as everyone else is not a good strategy. There is just not enough differentiation in the way each practice presents itself; the result is that too many architects are positioned in the marketplace as "just another architect" in search of *anybody* as a client. The only qualification that a potential client needs is a project to do right now.

Unfortunately, most architects are in search of anybody who will show up as a client. No matter what advertising (if any), marketing and promotion the firm is spending money and time doing, the efforts all tend to focus on "what we do." You could take various firms' brochures, cut out the names, mix them up and retape them, and it wouldn't change much. Most architects are competing in the same media, promoting their services in the same way, and competing for the same projects.

Because of the "sameness" of their efforts, the architects fight over limited clients and therefore suffer declining profits to get one project. In case this is not clear, this means that you have to do more work, in less time, to make the same money.

THE ALTERNATIVE: NICHE MARKETING

The contrary position to all of this sets out to make the architect unique in the market and in the client's perception. The architect sets out to attract a certain somebody, not just anybody.

The important concept to understand is that the "who" is more important than the "what" to avoid fighting for the same projects with other architects Most think in terms of marketing and promoting what their services are. In reality, great marketing is about "who" they are to the client. It is about finding a unique "who" that perceives the unique needs of the client, and crafting a message specifically for the clients desired.

You should strive to evoke in your clients a "that's for me" reaction. When they get mail or e-mail, they will see it to be of great specific interest to them. That's niche marketing – quite a contrast to what most architects do, which is to be all things to all people.

THIS LEADS TO BEING NOTHING TO EVERYONE.

The more specialized your niche, the better. Target marketing is efficient. For example, if you market to do office remodels, narrow your focus to a single specialty: You could place an ad in a magazine just for dentists and specifically target their needs. The "that's for me" reaction is there. (For a great example of niche practice, go to Page 206 and read the story of Jeff Peterson.)

Niche marketing will let you attract clients who are motivated, trusting, and will see you as the specialist and the expert authority. The best part is that this makes fee resistance go away since you are the expert "for them."

ARCHITECTURAL INSANITY #2:

THINKING LIKE AN ARCHITECT ALL THE TIME

You were brutally trained to act, speak, look, and think like architects because that is who you are. This was fine and dandy for getting through architectural school, great if you currently work in an architectural school, perfect for attending architectural meetings and when chewing the fat with other architects, but guess what....itit stinks when it comes to how you connect with your clients, especially when it comes to attracting new projects.

If you are going to be proficient at getting more projects that you want, you have to stop thinking like an architect about your marketing – or you have to employ marketing that wasn't developed by someone thinking like an architect. (whether they are or aren't an architect themselves....it makes no difference).

Architects and designers and people in our field are quite often guilty of acting high and mighty on marketing without taking into account what the message needs to say from the client's viewpoint. Clients write the check, so just maybe the marketing should speak to them more than to your peers. Architects usually miss the mark completely with their promoting messages and then are sorely disappointed in the poor results. Keep in mind that "Networking" doesn't count if it is not done in a very specific way.

In my marketing system, I show examples of ads from the 18th and 19th centuries that would outsell most of what is published in any Yellow Pages book today, let alone magazines or newspapers. How did we go so far off target and stop viewing the world from the client's perspective? When did we stop thinking about what they are searching for in the marketplace?

Architect, are you doing the same thing again and again and again? Are you upset with your results? Many architects fall into this trap unknowingly.

Not only do the marketing reps know little about effective marketing that really works (and remember, works means a verifiable return on investment), they also don't have a clue about what the architectural conditions and daily realities are for those clients who need your help.

Very few of these reps have been through construction with an architect (or even know anyone who has). Not only does make them ignorant, but the marketing they sell you doesn't have the right message at all. Instead of the marketing performing like a perfectly executed swan dive, it winds up doing a big belly flop in the public pond of messages, and somehow we are surprised when it does so.

If architects understood that they absolutely had to view their promotion from the client's perspective, a big light bulb would come on. They would fire those around them who don't "get it" (ad sales reps, graphic designers, etc.) and reap the huge financial benefits that would result from the changes in their marketing – and they would have more clients to help in the process.

One big reason the Architecture Marketing System works so well for architects is that it is written from the end user's (the client's) perspective – not from *your* perspective of "thinking like an architect," nor from the oblivious ad rep's perspective.

Until I figured this out, my marketing judgment often was clouded.."

Sometimes the "other" who puts the kibosh on a great marketing strategy is actually your "other half," who simply says, "I don't like your marketing." That happens a lot in professional practices, especially small ones.

Architect, unless your spouse is part of my training program or was a highly successful, full-time, direct-response marketer, he or she cannot give you helpful advice. Yes, your "other half" really does care about you but lacks the same bottom-line concern for putting projects into the practice.

Those projects ultimately put food on the table and clothes on the kids, pay for college, fund your retirement, and much more – all big reasons that you absolutely must spend wisely and see a huge return on your marketing investments for the sacrifice and hard work it takes to be an architect.

Yes, we like it when the image looks good and gets praise from our peers, but it is just not what it takes to get the projects and the results you want.

HERE'S THE BOTTOM LINE:

Turn off any "thinking like an architect" mentality, and you'll immediately see a change in how you view the world around your practice and what it *really* takes to design the right marketing message and strategies. By just doing this one action, you will shift your thinking in the right direction for more success with these projects on a regular basis.

ARCHITECTURAL INSANITY #3:

FAILURE TO WORK ON YOUR PRACTICE INSTEAD OF *IN* YOUR PRACTICE ALL THE TIME

No, this doesn't mean you are licking stamps and sealing envelopes, but it does mean you are making sure that the systems and marketing specifics are being carried out by you and your team members in the right manner so that they are effective and you get results.

I see this all the time with my new members and even the ones who have been in the Elite Architect Programs a long time: the temptation to only work in your practice and on your projects. I know, this is what you were trained for, but unfortunately you do need to stop working in your practice on a regular basis to actually work on your practice.

You need specific time allotted in your week to work on all the systems that need to be in place to ensure a continuous flow of new projects in the practice for you and your team to work on. This is for now until you don't have your own practice.

Success in your practice and in project acceptance involves more than just how you deliver options for a future project and how "really good" your construction documents are. (I've never heard architects saying their documents are not good). Many other steps and conditions that greatly affect acceptance rates happen back when a client is referred to your practice or comes into your practice via exterior marketing.

From that point forward, *every* detail along the way leading to the project acceptance affects your success or failure to indeed get the project. If you drop too many pieces of the puzzle, project acceptance is on its way to failure. The "devil is in the details," and most of your peers don't understand that. But it's what shoots down many projects, causes deep frustration, and ultimately results in fewer people getting the life-changing benefits that you, as the architect, are trained to deliver.

Yes, this requires that you take time in your weekly schedule to ensure that all those details are built the right way in your systems, that you have regular team meetings and ongoing reinforcement with your team. It is only worth it of course, if you want to increase your income and pick and chose which projects you will work on.

We have done a lot of groundwork, and you have spent years (possibly decades) learning to be a better architect. It is now time to shift the focus of your thinking so you can put more of those hard-earned architectural skills to use by helping more clients.

CHAPTER 4

What Are Your Strategies?

"In the land of the blind,
the one-eyed man is king."
Erasmus

STRATEGIC THINKING FOR ARCHITECTS

Today more than ever, wise architects are learning to focus their practices on what creates a winning life: professionally and personally, financially and emotionally. This requires a strategy that gives your clients/ prospects/ customers what they want and gives you and your practice the optimal profits and lifestyle you want – easier said over coffee than done.

What is strategy? It is the focusing of your limited resources cleverly to uniquely give your clients/ prospects/ customers what they want and give you the maximum profits: in finance, in gratification, and in lifestyle. Architecture has to be just as gratifying professionally as it is financially because it is not the kind of profession for the faint of heart and it is definitely long hours of work at the practice. Maybe you don't see it as work, but your aching eyes after a long day in front of drawings say that it is.

Here's the reality: It is no longer enough to just "show up and wait" for the success we all demand. There are too many variables. that have to be dealt with. It must be created intentionally, through a strategic plan and implementation of that plan to bring the end result. Creating or expanding on a niche in architecture, such as doing churches or luxury Mediterranean homes, requires strategic thinking.

Most architect owners around you and I are just doing things without an ongoing plan or strategy in hopes that something ("pretty please") will work. This is the "throw enough mud on the wall and see what sticks" approach. It's a phenomenon not limited to architects but rampant in the vast majority of small businesses all making the exact same mistake: Tactics, without a well-conceived strategy, result in wasted effort and money, confused staff, and limited effectiveness.

When thinking strategically about your firm, here's a guiding principle. The client wants the professional practice to give them more of what they want and less of what they don't want. Take a look at any currently-booming business (or older ones for that matter) and you'll find that fundamentally the clients get what they want.

Once you have a successful strategy created and in place, here's what else is critical to embrace: It never rests, it always needs attention, it will need adaptation, and all of that requires energy. Rust doesn't rest, so businesses can't either.

You need to find the tools to better articulate your strategy, to keep you energized as you move forward, and to help adapt to challenges. Stay ahead of the rest!

As long as you have your practice, this process never ends. You need a marketing system, project acceptance systems, and to be part of some implementation sessions to be able to leverage your time, effort, money and resources to put yourself well ahead of your competition and stay there.

Your strategy must avoid the pitfalls of learning from just your own experience. You want to avoid that emotional and financial pain. Clearly, for many, to be part of a membership elevates them far beyond what they would have accomplished on their own, no matter how long they toiled for it.

I get this question from my members regularly: "How do you come up with all those strategies, tools and ideas for my practice?" The answer is simple: I talk with a lot of your peers, do research, and participate in mastermind groups.

It's much easier to have a look at someone else's practice and see what they can do to improve their results. Think of it like this: When you look at your drawings too long, you just can't seem to find the right solution for your project. Then one of your peers walks by and tells you something simple that puts you right back on track.

NOT ALL STRATEGIES ARE EQUAL

This is worth repeating: Not all strategies are equal. It is the clever use of existing resources or resources that can be easily acquired that makes the biggest difference in creating a winning strategy. You can choose to cleverly acquire a knowledge base and tangible pieces of your strategy plan, with Architect Profits, for example.

If your strategies are unique and wanted by the public, it eliminates most marketing problems. I insist that members of my programs create a "Category of Number One" to help eliminate marketing issues with competitors. Such a winning strategy is far better than coping with one that isn't articulated – and you are indeed practicing a strategy even if it is not to think about one.

The best strategies are unique and difficult for others to duplicate, thereby protecting you from them. Your strategies should deal with particulars of what you and your clients desire. This requires *focus* and *concentration.*

Concentrate on giving your clients more of the things they want or removing what they don't want. What's important is not what you think they want; it's what they think. Be sure to ask them.

Eliminating simple things that they don't want or that frustrate them often will give you more leverage than adding things they want. For example, one of today's fast-growing franchises promises to eliminate the frustration of waiting for a plumber. They promise a plumber within an hour of your phone call. The marketing plays to something none of us want. No one wants to wait all day for a plumber to show up.

The franchise is booming and will continue to reap huge rewards as long as other companies do not grab the strategy and dilute the advantage. Because barriers to entry are not that high, the odds are this advantage in plumbing will disappear quite rapidly.

Here is an example of an advantage that disappeared: Ten to fifteen years ago, green architecture was seen as unique and special. The public didn't know much about it. Still, some wanted to decrease the negative impact on the environment. The earliest adopting architects got the de-facto role of "green specialists." In most markets, that early advantage disappeared as many others hoisted the banner of green architect, diluting the term's value. Now "green architect" is in the same useless language land of non-differentiation as "good design" architecture.

No matter what area you focus on, establishing yourself as *the* authority in your area of concentration in the eyes of the public should be part of that strategy. But be aware, as we'll see in a minute, that what makes you that authority for your prospects is not accumulating courses and letters after your name.

"Education is a progressive discovery of our ignorance."
Will Durant

CE, CREDENTIALS, AND CLIENTS

You know what the problem is with credentials of any kind and piling up massive amounts of continuing education? Clients don't understand any of it. It's a basic assumption that you are "keeping up." Indeed, you need to keep up with your education to be able to stay registered as an architect. You have to do it; it's a given.

The reality is that all the courses that you take and the letters after your name are gibberish to most people outside architecture. They just see a bunch of letters that really don't mean a whole lot to them. Sorry, but LEED Accredited means nothing to most people outside our field, and forget FAIA, RA, ASLA or NCARB. I've even run across architects who thought the letters P.C. or L.L.C. were academic titles.

Yet architects often kid themselves about what those letters can do for them. And it isn't magic! The letters are great, but they aren't what get clients to know and trust you and spend tens of thousands of dollars with you. In fact, if those letters have gone to your head a little too much and you've entered "pompous-architect" land, I can tell you the letters have now become a hindrance.

Let me ask you this: Do you really know the meaning of all the letters that your doctor has after his or her name? Of all the different specialists you have seen over your lifetime? You're probably like me: not at all, but you still went with their recommendation. I recently had sinus surgery and never even thought of looking at the meaning of the different qualifications after the name of my surgeon – and she put me to sleep for the surgery.

The harsh reality is that you can have more continuing education or credentials than 90 percent of those architects around you, yet clients are just as likely to pick someone with none. That is unless you go to direct and focused efforts to combat this non-understanding of training/credentials.

Here is one well-kept secret: The best place to get this done is when you include this information in your marketing and project acceptance systems after the client has contacted you.

If you help them understand what all those things mean in ways that matter to them and that they will find important in their industry language, it directly contributes to whether a client picks you and to whether more projects go forward. As architects, you need to maintain credits to stay registered as an architect, but clients don't make decisions that way.

If getting more projects and having more clients select you over all the rest sounds appealing, then it's critical to understand this concept *and* make sure the client gets the information about your training and credentials at a level that is understandable. Because other local architects don't understand this strategy, you can move past them – even if they have more architectural qualifications than you. Architects who take this to heart routinely report that it's one more piece of the "new project" puzzle whose discovery was worth its weight in gold.

ONE OF A KIND: YOUR EXPERT STATUS

For the highly trained architect, putting together a specific combination of training, credentials, and talents so that you are one of a kind in your market is one of the best ways to fight the "all architects are the same" problem that exists in the marketplace.

Architects are all the same in the client's eyes, registered architect or not, and anyone who doesn't recognize this and then goes to efforts to set the practice apart fails to understand basic human nature and deserves the comparison.

Being seen as the "go-to" expert or the "wizard" is a direct side effect of not only building your one-of-a-kind status but of understanding that the deliberate promotion of such status at every turn is necessary.

It's critical to understand that declaring yourself "expert" is not the same as saying "I'm the best," a phrase that most boards frown upon and that doesn't resonate well with clients. One can declare, "The most recognized expert in ABC-ville" without needing to state "I'm the best." The client infers that; you don't need to say it.

Here are just a few items on a very long list that will automatically help put you in that Category of Number One, especially when attached to your unique work flow (your method) of architecture: extremely low number of change orders, all projects on time/on schedule, speed of delivery, architectural promises and warranties, providing interior/architectural/landscape services under one roof, etc.

EVEN MORE REASONS FOR BEING THE WIZARD:

Three BIG reasons:

1. It makes more of your competition irrelevant. Yes, I know what many architects think: "I'm competing against (insert your favorite rant/program/consumer thing here)." But here's the truth: Out of the people who are actually purchasing architectural services, some of them will consider competitors – so why not eliminate as much of that as possible?

2. It makes it harder to cost-compare. Again, apples to apples means commodity pricing – very bad for you. On the other end, comparing apples to oranges means very difficult to cost-compare (basically impossible) – very good for you.

3. It allows fees appropriate to the skill level and for all the stuff that is required to be in the Category of One delivering something unique. For most, this means fees that are significantly higher than competitors', even in difficult economic times.

BE ONE OF A KIND – FOREVER

As time passes and technology, materials, and techniques come and go, another aspect of understanding is that part of your evaluation of whatever is "new" is to be asking "How does this keep me in the Category of One?" Again, you need to make sure that anything "new" is always described for and discussed with clients in ways that mean something to them – not just to you or your team.

WHO WILL DECLARE YOU THE "WIZARD"?

Certainly, you need to have credentials and a package of services and methods that make you unique and the specialist. That's a given. So, you have all those things, now what? Who's going to say, "Ms. Smith, YOU are the expert here in Dusseldorf!"?

Here's another big secret: Take a look in the mirror. It's up to you to declare your expert status via your promotional materials and marketing that the public will see and to tell your clients and potential clients about it at every possible chance.

Yes, if you happen to be at the pinnacle of the entire profession (I will not name any "star-chitects" here because we all have a different opinion on who is or is not), you will get declared an expert by your peers and you won't have to do it yourself (or maybe not). Just realize the kind of work it takes to be put into that category.

If you wait for your colleagues to make such a declaration, chances are really good that you'll be waiting more than your lifespan. Even if you get lucky and your local architects do declare you an expert after a few decades of meetings at your favorite associations, you'll have thrown away most of your peak years of practice. Don't chance it. Declare it yourself.

I can hear it already: Some might think that it is time to raise the branding flag of recognition. Let's take a closer look, or should I say a unique look, at what your brand can really do for you, Mr. Architect.

WHAT IS YOUR BRAND?

THREE IMPORTANT TRUTHS ABOUT ARCHITECTURAL BRANDING

Many national consultants feel "mission statements," "branding" and "logos" are some of the most important aspects of your marketing efforts. You'll never hear anyone at Architect Profits saying such.

There are fundamental truths about branding and "image" that are not getting shared with architects. Buckle you seatbelt because this is going to be a bit of a shock, quite different from what you've been told before. Here they are:

TRUTH #1: MISSION STATEMENTS

Your clients could care less. Clients (actually everyone) are tuned to their favorite station whose call letters are WII-FM (what's in it for me). If you don't provide an answer to this question, you will have a hard time finding new projects.

Here are five things clients want instead of framed mission statements:

1. They want no problems.
2. They want to understand you, in simple terms.
3. They want options (but not too many).
4. They want the wizard.
5. They want respect.

TRUTH #2: LOGOS AND BRANDS

Logos? The only thing less important to your client than your logo is your mission statement. Thus, there is no need to worry too much about your logo design. A logo can cost from hundreds to thousands of dollars.

Instead of spending a month's marketing budget on your logo, invest this amount of money on direct response based marketing to make the phone ring with clients you wish to work with.

Logos can be useful if they grace a popular product on a shelf, backed by multimillions in advertising. *Then* there's value. When that level of money is spent, even when dead, a brand still has value.

Is that your situation? Is that the situation of even the largest architectural firms in the world? Doubtful. Think about it: Can you name three firms or one architect's logo right now? I'm sure your answer is no.

A logo can also be useful when a niche culture or sub-culture wear it on a polo shirt. In triathlons races, I've seen IronMan® logos tattooed on some fellow racers. That's true power in branding. No one is queuing up to get my logo as a tattoo – not even me!

Logos won't make or break your marketing efforts at getting the projects you want for your practice. Clients don't lie awake eagerly anticipating your newest logo design (or really any company's). The client simply doesn't care.

Still not convinced? A few years ago, people on the street were shown the logo of a well known restaurant chain– the real one and four fakes, all on the same sheet of paper. Despite the millions in franchise fees annually spent on marketing, only 6 percent could pick the real logo.

Architect logos backed by $50,000 to $300,000 are not going to beat that dismal result or create projects.

TRUTH #3: THE ARCHITECT IS *THE* BRAND

That's the case especially when you are performing very specialized projects or highly visible ones.

The more money involved in a project, the more important the YOU becomes. Clients need "who" you are, not "what" you are, and you in the meeting room are *the* brand. This becomes even more important after the client receives promotional information from the practice and schedules a meeting.

With the right marketing, clients can call a practice, know very little about the architect, and still be powerfully motivated to seek work with that office because they were offered solutions to problems, not logos, brands, or mission statements. Are you offering solutions to problems or simply wasting time, energy, and money on things the client doesn't care much about?

Let me be clear here. I am not saying you should not have a logo and a mission statement; you need to have one. What I'm saying is that you should not expect to get a project from it. I do have a logo for my company, and you should have one as well. Just don't spend too much of your time, energy and money on it, especially if you are just starting your practice. People know and remember you for who you are, not because you have a good-looking logo.

As far as your mission statement, it is important for YOU to know what it is so you can have a clear direction for your practice and to be sure you are staying on track. But don't expect people to remember what it is. I challenge you to tell me the mission statement of any of the top 10 biggest firms in this country. What? You don't know any of them? I think you get my point.

ESTABLISHING DIALOGUE WITH YOUR FUTURE CLIENT

Here is what you can do to effectively bring awareness to your future client with all the money you just saved. Returning home from a busy day, a potential client opens his mailbox and his interest is immediately drawn to a well-organized mailing explaining the potential benefits of using your services.

A creative postal campaign that speaks to the needs of your potential client base can start a dialogue, providing targeted messages based upon clients' particular needs. Properly planned postal "drip marketing" (in an organized sequence) can inform, delight and reach out to a targeted audience to build awareness of your services and your one-of-a-kind status.

To set yourself apart from the competition, it's important to craft a marketing strategy that creates positive awareness among your existing and prospective client base. Crafting the proper message and design can ensure that your message will stand out among your peers and will develop YOU as your brand.

Since mail is generally read at the end of the day, generally in a quieter place away from the daily rush of work, you have a prime opportunity to reach out to prospective clients who are receptive to messages from superior products and services.

Creating a message that focuses on piquing a prospective customer's interest can begin to establish the dialogues that lead to customer acquisition.

After you have established initial awareness for YOU as your brand, high-quality drip mailings help establish trust and generate momentum for your firm. Segmenting your client base according to their particular needs can ensure you send out messaging that will speak to them on a personal level, as opposed to spending money on trying to have people talk about you.

We'll see later on in the book how you can use the very same lessons from off-line campaigns and apply them to effective online targeted marketing: by providing customers with add-on value in terms of information and discounts, you'll cultivate the relationships that drive your business growth.

But before you start spending some of your money on these strategies, it would be wise to take a closer look at two critical tools that you already have but too often are underutilized in most offices: your phone and your website.

CHAPTER 5

The Importance of Your Phone

"We are what we repeatedly do. Excellence, therefore, is not an act but a habit."
Aristotle

The next two chapters will cover two of the most critical non-architectural tools in your practice when it comes to getting the clients and projects you want from your promotional efforts: your phone and your website. Those two crucial tools are often the missing link between your expensive professional skills and actually using those skills on real projects.

Let's start with the vital piece of equipment that is the telephone.

Here's the sad truth about your phone: You can be highly skilled, beautifully equipped, have top-notch staff, run killer ads and second-to-none marketing campaigns, and STILL miss out on new projects *if people aren't trained to use the phone correctly.*

If the phone isn't working right, you'll have:

- far fewer first meetings getting scheduled.
- more surprise "cancellations" happening.
- overall far fewer projects going forward.
- less return on your investment.

That first phone interaction before or after all your correct marketing, screening and qualifying can literally be either the deal maker or the deal breaker, as can the correct follow-up.

Because the phone is a critical component in making architecture practices successful, this next chapter of the book is entirely devoted to your phone line.

YOUR MARKETING LINE

Remember your telephone is the one tool that opens or closes the door to the practice. It must be used well. Why?

Nothing else matters if your phone is not answered well, so that prospective clients will schedule and keep meetings instead of calling someone else.

Remember, first impressions matter. The first voice that the potential client hears impacts how you are thought of. If your phone isn't handled well, the gate is closed and this potential client will call someone else. No marketing you do will matter after that.

People will either call directly your office from the Yellow Pages, your website, from a referral, or as a result of any of your marketing efforts. In general, people call several - firms to ask a first round of questions and then call back one or two to have a one-on-one meeting. This is your chance to show that you are different and that you are The One.

Being nice on the phone isn't enough. Being nice AND effective at getting what you want from the phone call by using the correct language is what is required for success in turning as many calls as possible into consults and projects.

We tend to think that only one employee is in charge of answering the phone at any time. But that person does go to lunch, meetings and other things. Therefore other people will also touch the phone and also need to be trained at getting better results from the phone.

WHAT TO DO: MEASURE

You can only improve what you can measure. How do you measure? Keep a phone log. The team/person in charge of the phone will probably say, "Why use a phone log? I know when there is a new prospect calling."

Yes, that was before you started to market your services properly, or at all. There was no reason to have one before; now, you need one. Actually, it would have been good for you to have had one before, you just didn't know.

You can use a plain spiral notebook. It need not be fancy. Write down every call. It is a good idea to have a specific phone line like an 800 number dedicated to your marketing efforts. It makes it easier to know when a potential client is calling and to track which piece of marketing is working or not. (Hmm, what a novel concept!)

First you need to record the date, time, name of caller, caller's contact information, team member who took the call, result, and dates for any follow-ups.

SCREENING SYSTEM

The phone line is also a very good tool when you have an ad in the newspaper to control all the calls coming in at the same time. You can easily have a specific voice mail message to help screen calls and ask people to "clearly" leave their information so you can call them back. This way you won't waste time trying to answer all those calls coming in at the same time or late at night, and it will be more productive overall for everyone this way.

On a regular basis, you look at the log to see what is happening and who is calling you. You will use the log to identify questions and answers you need to have ready. It can help identify new written systems and scripts needed for answering the phone based on the marketing piece used at that specific time.

This will help in providing the best possible answers to people calling for information. For example you will need to say something different if your marketing piece focuses on Green Architecture compared to a piece that focuses on End-of -Year Deadline.

WHY WOULD YOU USE SCRIPTS?

The purpose of a script is really to prepare for the delivery of your sales presentation, which begins when your telephone rings and, of course, begins with making the appointment. for your first meeting with the prospect. Think of a script as an organized presentation.

"If you fail to prepare, then you prepare to fail!"

Unfortunately, most coordinators today are coached on how to answer the questions of the prospective client when they call, but they are not coached on how to sell the appointment, which is really the ultimate goal when a prospect calls your office for the first time. You want to ensure that the prospect books a meeting with you; otherwise, the prospect will call somewhere else and forget about you. In other types of businesses, those who answer the phone would be called "order takers."

To be an expert at getting the appointment and to be sure that the prospect doesn't feel the need to call another firm, you or the person answering the phone in your office need to be prepared, organized, focused and understand sales. The way you become great at this is to practice it all the time.

I used to be the answering "voice" on the phone at my first job in a small firm in St. Louis because my boss liked my "French accent." My boss thought it sounded more "international." He never once told me what I should be doing when a prospect would call for the first time. That's not the smartest strategy, especially when people call with a specific accent that in this case was very different from mine.

Napoleon Hill, author of "The Law of Success," said that the only way you will get through life and get what you want is to sell your way through life.

Many practices fail not because of poor management but because they decided that once they were in business, they didn't have to sell or do any marketing since after all, they are professionals and professionals don't do that. (Think about law firms; they sure do a lot of advertising and sure start their "timer" as soon as they pick up the phone.) Many architects think that for some magic reason people will just come to them.

At the end of the day, all that really matters in your practice is this: What did you sell? What did each of your team members sell? Getting really good at writing scripts and actually using them will very quickly improve your bottom line, with no additional cost in your marketing efforts, just by improving how the phone is answered on a first-call basis.

One of the biggest misconceptions about using scripts is that it's a tool that only telemarketing sharks use – those people who call you at night while you're eating dinner or early on a Sunday morning to sell you something you don't want. They read the scripts word for word while sounding and acting just like a robot.

They don't take a breath; they don't even wait to see if you have a question. Many times they don't even know that you've already hung up.

Don't worry! You're not that kind of business. Now you know that sales is customer service and customer service is sales. Sales is a tool, a skill for life, a communication tool, and without it in business you'll fail and you'll be out of business. Keep in mind that the people in this case are calling you, not the other way around.

11 REASONS TO USE A SCRIPT

1. We're human: We forget what we're going to say, we get confused, and we can become tired, especially toward the end of the day.

2. We wander off track and we get interrupted.

3. Scripts keep you focused on the essentials of a particular call.

4. Scripts are your rule book; they are how to capture and maximize your ROI (return on investment) and your ROE (return on effort).

5. You get systemized with scripts.

6. Scripts guide you on how to guide the call down the path of making the appointment, which is the sale that will lead to a new project.

7. Scripts help you to continue positioning yourself as the expert during the entire phone conversation.

8. Scripts guide you on how to close the prospective client versus the client closing you. You must control the call; otherwise, the client will.

9. Scripts help you to prevent unnecessary schmoozing and get you and the caller back to business.

10. Scripts have many different uses: inbound calls to set appointments, confirming appointments, project presentation, project acceptance, handling disgruntled clients, etc.

11. Many times the architect is resistant to using scripts because the team is running the show and the practice. The architect doesn't want to rock the boat with the staff. This is really wrong and an entirely different topic for another time. Decide who's running the show; use scripts.

ONE MORE TIME: WHY IS THE PHONE SO IMPORTANT?

The phone is the most important instrument in the practice. The only three things more important are the architect's ability to practice and his or her two hands; the four most important things in the practice aren't even books or pieces of technology. That's REAL money that pays team members' salaries, bonuses, 401(k)s, and other benefits.

Here is an example outside your field that shows why the phone is so important. Not that long ago I decided to convert my mountain bike into a road bike. So I called a small local shop in my neighborhood.

A woman at the shop picked up the phone and asked me what I needed. I said that I wanted to convert my bike. First thing she said was that the shop was very busy and that it would take at least two weeks to look at my bike. She asked how much money I was planning on spending. I told her between $300 and $400, to which she said, "Yeah, that's about right," and told me to call back when I would be ready to bring my bike. I was so surprised that I said okay, and she hung up on me.

I then called the big bike store here in town. The guy who picked up the phone said I could bring my bike in that day so the shop could have a look at it and help me pick out the new parts. Based on the changes, he said, the shop would let me know when it could be done.

So guess which one of the two stores I decided to go with? The one that told me to come right away. I ended up spending much more money than I had originally planned.

Here are some statistics that also might convince you of the importance of your phone. You should also keep this information in mind for your next presentation in front of a potential client.

To be a truly effective communicator, your body language and tone of voice must be consistent with your content. Even the most powerful words spoken in a monotone with lifeless body language will fail to rouse anyone – better make sure you have great pictures at hand.

In a study at UCLA, Dr. Albert Mahrabian found that when verbal, vocal and visual signals are inconsistent, content counts for a mere 7 percent of the overall message. In such a situation, 55 percent of the message is transmitted by facial expression and body language; 38 percent comes from voice quality – pitch, tone, volume and inflection. All those things have an even greater impact when you are not in front of a potential client, but on the phone.

So, when you think about it, when you are meeting with a person that you want to influence, especially for the first time, a warm, friendly smile, a firm handshake and good eye contact can work wonders. But if anything about your voice is flat or distracting, annoying or boring, you've just reduced your effectiveness by 38 percent.

As you can see, the way your phone is answered has a huge impact when people call your office for the first time. Don't mess it up!

THE BASIC OVERVIEW FOR YOUR PHONE

1. When a call comes in, a "phone slip" is filled out with all of the potential client's information entered on it. It contains vital information as well as the architectural motivators, the real reasons they decided to call you that specific day.

2. There are two goals with every phone call: to schedule a phone consult AND to obtain information for future marketing and follow-up. Nothing else matters.

3. Getting mailing information and a phone number is paramount. Do not allow a client to hang up without giving you this information if at all possible.

WHAT HAPPENS AFTER AN INBOUND PHONE CALL REQUEST?

1. After a phone call, enter each potential client, regardless of whether he or she made a consult, into a master New Projects Excel database. Also enter and document "where" they came from, meaning the marketing source (exactly: website, newsprint, magazine, postcard, flyer, etc.).

2. The New Projects Database is the separate database unrelated to your accounting/insurance software/ practice management software. This allows an entire list of potential clients to continue to grow and be subject to your marketing. Over time, some of these clients will be "ready" to have their dream project. If your practice

kept in touch with them, then they will be more likely to go through with their project development with your firm.

3. If a consult was made, then the opportunity slip goes into the client's folder along with a New Project tracking sheet.

4. If the consult wasn't made, then the inbound opportunity slip goes into the follow-up binder for follow-up seven to ten days later. It is crucial to do the task and be nice so that the prospect will remember you upon deciding to go ahead with a project. After each contact ages past a month, move it out of the "current category" and file by date (newest to oldest) into the greater than one month category.

With every request for information, no matter how it arrives at the office, live or via email or voice mail, only two possible things have happened to that potential client. Either a consult was made or it was not made. Using a follow-up binder ensures that you have consistent follow-up for all the clients requesting information and that scripts and materials to prepare for the calls and handle the calls are in front of the team member performing the follow-up.

WHAT'S THE BIG DEAL ABOUT FOLLOW-UP?

Practices, like yours, that spend sums of time and money on external marketing must follow up. In fact, if you look at the money spent on marketing and the average project size of the potential client who calls being worth tens of thousands of dollars in production, you can't afford NOT to follow up. Most practices never follow up, and this is a good thing for you: It's an easy way to position yourself in the Category of Number One.

Back to my bike story: Did the lady from the small shop call me back to get my job? Nope, even though I had told her I wanted to give her my money!

THE FACTS:

A client with a serious desire to have a project done by an architect often had those problems (desires) develop over many years, way before deciding to make that call that specific day. Clients enter and exit states of being ready for starting a project due to multiple factors in their daily lives (some architectural, most not architectural at all).

Every client is on a roller-coaster ride called life, and it's impossible to guess whether a client is on the "fun" part of the ride, or it's one of those times when life gets in the way of plans – such as the need for an architect.

Few architects understand the importance of this, even though it greatly impacts thoughts and specific "to do's" related to marketing and project acceptance both near and long term!

For some practices the lack of follow-up is the difference between success and failure at having enough ongoing "yes" answers from new projects to make the ROI high enough so that the entire effort of seeking clients makes sense. These also include the practices that experiment with problem-solution marketing that don't plug the prospective client inquiries into a short- and long-term projects acceptance system. I'm not even going to talk about the "good old times" where the phone would just ring with new projects to pick from. Forget about it; this is not coming back.

THE BOTTOM LINE:

As time passes, some clients will enter the project phase with your firm, IF they continue to hear from your practice via follow-up. When does the follow-up end? Easy. When the client buys, dies, or says, "Take me off your list."

This process will create your marketing funnel, which is the systematic process by which potential clients contact your practice and get out of it as a happy client or not a client at all. A rule in marketing is that the higher priced the product, the longer the funnel. Since construction and architectural services command higher fees, the funnel is indefinite in length. The motto for your architectural marketing funnel is that potential clients who inquire either "buy, die, move away, or beg to get off your list." This means that once they enter your system, they will receive information from you virtually forever.

The reality is that there is a high cost to reaching out to new prospects, contacting and maintaining a list of potential clients who may never work with your firm – that they are balanced by the clients who do. This list of potential clients who continuously hear from you will be predisposed to choose your firm over others because of this contact that started from that very first call.

One important benefit that you will gain with your follow-up with the people who have raised their hands by contacting you that first time is that you will at the same time create your own followers of potential clients, people who will gladly get information from you because they like you. This is also known as your "herd" in the marketing world, and there is a great example of how powerful this can be in the third section of this book. This will result in much easier and satisfying relationships with those future clients since the trust in you has been established for a long time.

As you can see now, your phone is really one of the most critical tools in your office, and results can easily and greatly improve when the phone is used and handled the right way. And all these benefits come at an extremely low cost for your practice.

Now that we have covered this first door to your practice, let's take a closer look at another tool that is extremely important but often badly used by most architectural firms: your website.

CHAPTER 6

The Importance of Your Website

"You either make money or make excuses"
Ryan Hunter

Now that you understand how important your phone is, it's time to focus on your website. That is taking for granted that you do have one. Do you? Like most business owners, I understand the importance of the website for people to find us, and I want to feel good about it when people click on it.

Unfortunately, or fortunately, depending on how you want to see it, there is a big difference between looks and what works. I know how much time is put into developing and keeping the best website first hand. That's why it's a shame to see architects with websites that are ineffective, or worse, actually drive away potential clients.

Let's start with eye-opening research that just came out just a few years ago called "First Impressions Count for Web" published in the journal Behavior and Information Technology by a Canadian team from Carleton University. This study shows that the first impressions count for Internet users, who make up their minds about the quality of a website in the blink of an eye. Really.

These researchers found that the brain makes decisions on websites in just a 20th of a second of viewing the first page of a website. To put this amount of time in perspective, this is three or four times faster than your fastest muscle reflex.

They were surprised as they believed it would take at least ten times longer to form an opinion.

What's really critical about their research is that they also revealed that the first impressions have a lasting impact on how people perceive your website. If they don't like it right then, they won't like it once they read your information or look at your images. So we are really talking about speedy conclusions here, no kidding.

Here is how they did the research. The Canadian team showed volunteers glimpses of websites, lasting for only 50 milliseconds. The volunteers then had to rate the websites in terms of their aesthetic appeal.

The researchers found that the quickly formed conclusions closely matched with the final opinions of the websites that had been made after much longer periods of examination from those people.

Even the lead researcher of the paper, Gitte Lindgaard, expressed her surprise at the results, saying that her colleagues believed it would be impossible to really see anything in that amount of time. But the results showed that the judgments were being formed almost as quickly as the eye could take in information.

A few years ago I took a speed reading class which, to me, explains a bit how this is possible. The strategy of the class was to "flip" through the book first. Meaning you would just stare at the middle of the book and then flip page by page nonstop until the end of the book for a few times to let it sink into your brain. After a few days, you go back to the book and search for relevant information that you need. Obviously that works for information books, not so much for books you want to enjoy on vacation.

I have to say that it does work. At first I was very skeptical, but the teacher explained that it was the same as when you enter a new place looking for something specific – such as the restroom in a restaurant. You don't look at details, like what the tables are made of, or how many people are at the tables to your right. You just take it all in. Your brain is obviously extremely fast.

The researchers also believe that these quickly-formed first impressions last because of what is known to psychologists as the "halo effect." If people believe a website looks good, then this positive quality will spread to other areas, such as the website's content. Since people like to be right, even people outside architecture, they will continue to use the website that made a good first impression, as this will further confirm that their initial decision was a good one.

So what is it that you need to take out of this study? Well, obviously unless the first impression is a positive one, your prospect will be out of your site before they even know that you might be offering better services than your competitors. To avoid instant rejection, the most important elements of a landing page (the home page, not the "skip intro" page) are your headline and your overall page design. And what I mean by this is that it needs to be simple, clear, and straight to the point.

If your landing page just has nothing on it, you're done. If it takes too much time to load, you're toast. If it's confusing and the text is too small to read, this will mean too much work for the person looking at your website, and it's not going to work.

Basically, there are two main reasons to have a website: to sell something or to capture the person's information to sell something later. In your case it is to sell your services. It is not enough to have a "pretty," "cool," or "fancy" website; you need to have a way to get what you want out of it. Otherwise, you are wasting your time and your money.

KEEP IN MIND, YOUR WEBSITE IS NOT A SHRINE TO YOUR GREATNESS

Let's start with the first critical point here: It is amazing that some firms still don't have a website. There is no reason not to have one, none. You can easily have one done by some online-website companies that you can find on the Internet; there is no need to have a fancy one. It's actually the other way around: Fancy-looking websites just confuse people.

For example, look at Frank Gehry's website. It's only three pages: home page, career page and contact page. Of course, most people know who is he, but the point is that you don't need to have a complicated website. You just need one. The investment can be really low with really high results.

In one of our surveys, one of the frustrations that architects mentioned time after time was how difficult it is to find good new employees. Don't be fooled, the good ones will look for your website and just go to the next firm if you don't have one. And chances are really high that most potential clients will be looking at information on a website first before contacting a firm. You need to get on board!

WHAT YOU SHOULD CONSIDER

Now that we've covered this critical "detail," here are eight points you should consider doing to boost your website effectiveness immediately:

1. MAKE SURE YOUR SITE LOADS *QUICKLY*

Now that we understand that the website needs to do its job right in the first second that someone clicks on it, let's look at the ".1/1/10 second" rule. For the last 30 years, the research (on radio, TV and the Web) has been consistent on this:

- People consider any delay below 1/10th of a second to be "instantaneous."
- People will stay focused if the delay is below 1 second.
- They will move on to the next site with any delay over 10 seconds.

No doubt the 10-second number is getting even shorter these days. Watch your own behavior at a website. If an expensive "flash" website is taking more than a few seconds to load, you'll move on to something else. Your potential clients will do the same if you have that kind of website. Remember, they don't know how great your website is and won't care to wait to find out.

The big one that I see again and again is how long it takes to upload the pictures on some architect's websites. For some it's really quick; others take forever. An easy fix is to reduce the resolution of your images.

2. KEEP THE GOOD STUFF "ABOVE THE FOLD"

"Above the fold" is a newspaper term. Advertisers have known for a long time that ads do better when they are placed above the newspaper fold. In today's cyber-world, that term has come to mean the space on a web page that is first visible when the page loads, without needing to scroll down.

"Above the Fold" is precious real estate. Yet take a look at most websites: that space is taken by large banners and meaningless graphics, or plain nothing. It usually "looks" good but has nothing to say to the potential client about why you are better than any other firm. As far as architects' pages, there is usually nothing. Also keep in mind that this rule holds true for all pages of your website.

Think about it: How many magazines have no headline on the cover page? Very few, and there is a good reason for it: It's better to have one.

3. GET RID OF ANY "INTRODUCTION" PAGE!

This is a favorite among web designers. (You know – those people with an art degree, whose highest calling is not to pay the bills in a small business but instead to win art awards from other artists.)

Hence the dramatic introduction pages, also known as a splash screen. It might be all black with a couple words in the center. Or it might be an animation that fills the screen, except for a tiny link that says "Skip Intro."

Your web designer is going to fight you on this, but you now know better. Don't fall for the rationale that you have to "set the mood." This is not a date. This is business.

4. USE PICTURES THE RIGHT WAY

It's no contest: Studies of eye tracking on websites prove that pictures are by far the most interesting items on a page. (I bet you will look at the picture at No.5 before finishing this section!!!)

And where does the eye go, immediately after looking at a picture? It goes right beneath the picture. Most websites waste that space with either no caption, or a meaningless one.

Instead of "Joe Smith, AIA," your caption should read "Joe Smith, the most reliable green architect" or whatever other short, benefit-laden message you want to impart. Very few people know about eye-tracking studies, and fewer yet actually apply the findings.

Another critical point about images: Most architects use images that people outside our field cannot understand. You can use the pictures you want, but if one isn't easy to understand, be sure to clearly explain it in words.

5. MAKE AN OFFER

One of the very best maxims in effective marketing is "Give Before You Get." In this case, what you should be giving is a special report or another offer to help prospects want you AND give you their information so you can

Go back to #4

contact them at a later time if they are not ready to work with you.

It might be "How to Choose the Best Architect for Your New House" or "How You Can Stop Wasting Your Money by Turning Green." An important thing to remember: More and more people give "free reports" of any kind. To set yourself apart, you need to show an actual picture of your free report cover so the potential client knows it is a truly professional one.

Giving such a report to your website visitors does a few things:

- It establishes you as an expert.
- It separates you from other architectural offices, which give nothing.
- Since you will ask for the person's information, you will be able to follow up.
- It helps to dispel myths about architecture.
- It can be passed around to others, creating yet more projects.

6. DON'T STRESS YOUR READERS, OR THEY WON'T READ

Online readers are usually pressed for time and multi-tasking (while at work). If your website takes a lot of work to get through, most people won't bother.

Here's what I define as work:

- Too-small print.
- Unusual typefaces
- Too-long lines
- Big blocks of text
- Low-contrast type

Here is an example: Most architects like a nice block of text on their website; it's "prettier." Studies show that when you do this, it makes it harder to read for your prospect. Look at a magazine; it has much more than text blocks, and they aren't big ones.

7. MAKE THE SITE ABOUT YOUR CLIENTS, NOT YOU.

Think how you label the buttons on your website. Now think from the clients' perspective, meaning what kind of information they are looking for … for themselves. What do you see?

For instance, don't call it "Client Education." Nobody wants to be "educated." Call it "Ask the Architect," or "Frequently Asked Questions." Don't call it "Our Expertise," call it "What Can Be Done For You." Don't call it "Our Philosophy" or "Our Mission." Remember, no one cares about your or my philosophy or mission. Instead, call it "How We're Different" or even "Why Our Clients Keep Coming Back."

8. INSERT TESTIMONIALS

People are social creatures. That's why testimonials (i.e., social proof) have such great power. You should have a testimonial on your home page, and on every other page if possible. Plus, it needs to say more than "J.C." for the name. You can say "Janice C., Peoria IL" and still maintain confidentiality.

Why is this important? Because people don't believe "J.C." is a real person. The more information you provide, the more real the testimonial will appear, and the more effect it will have. And if you can have a picture of the client with his or her project, it's even better for the result. Refer to the section on testimonials to find out how easy it is to get plenty of great ones from your preferred clients. Also be sure to include endorsement from other architects and people you work with. The same goes for any publication you might have for any of your projects. You need to make sure people see it.

HOW TO MAKE YOUR TESTIMONIALS COUNT

Let's spend a few minutes on the concept of testimonials because of its importance. I'm guessing it started back in wooly mammoth times: the tendency of people to look to other people for reassurance. On one level they judge for themselves that wooly mammoth meat is worth eating. On another level they want to hear the other cave people first grunt their approval. Human nature hasn't changed all that much in the 21st century. People are still very highly influenced by others' opinions. Therefore the testimonial is one of the most powerful techniques you can use to attract and retain clients.

Caution: States vary in what they allow architects and other professionals to use in the way of testimonials. In fact, some states are stuck in prehistoric mindsets; thus, please check your state rules and accept or ignore my advice below, depending on those rules. The Federal Trade Commission allows you to edit testimonials as long as you preserve the client's meaning. If done carefully, it's usually OK to shorten and smooth out testimonials. Do not make up testimonials! You should have a file with each testimonial, accompanied by the client's agreement to use that testimonial and the text provided to you.

The more specificity, the better. For example, an ineffective testimonial would be: "I recommend Ms. Smith." A solid testimonial would be: "I was initially skeptical that I would get the project I've always dreamed of, but the result is actually better than my wildest dream … and the project was on time and on budget! Ms. Smith and her team made it easy throughout the process."

Please note something else in that last testimonial – a reference to skepticism. Some of the most powerful testimonials refer to someone's doubt, fear, or skepticism and how it was proven unnecessary. Such testimonials sound far more realistic than the cheerleader who only expresses gushing enthusiasm for the architect.

As you collect more testimonials, try to get ones that address a specific concern or feature. That way, you can have an "on budget" testimonial on your web page that talks about fees, a "first-class process" testimonial on the page describing your team, and so on.

With just a bit of planning, your testimonials can keep working for you for years to come, continually reassuring website visitors that they're making a smart choice to book an appointment to see you.

WHEN LESS IS MORE

I just mentioned that it is in your best interest to be as specific as possible when it comes to your testimonials, and same is true with your overall website. Let me explain why.

We can all agree on one thing: Each year we're bombarded with more media clamoring for our attention. Websites, text messages, Facebook messages, electronic billboards, televisions in elevators, you name it, with the next invasion just around the corner.

Problem #1: More distractions mean ever-smaller attention spans on the part of your clients.

Problem #2: Most architectural practices think in parallel, while most clients think serially. Practices structure their websites with too many types of services on a page and too many decisions for any one client. At the same time, clients tend to have one dominant thought at a time: "My project can't be too expensive," or "I can't decide what I really want," or "Can you do something about my house remodel?"

If you try to make one web page address all those needs, you're likely to address none of them adequately. At the other end of the spectrum, if you say nothing on your page, it is a big waste. Unmotivated people who are merely browsing will think in general terms. For instance, they may search for "architect." But motivated clients are more specific in their searches and have already looked for "best architect for house remodel." They will have already Googled multiple websites and now want to know more specific information about "alternative construction," "new products and finishes," and so on.

The bottom line is that you should not have a one-size-fits-all web page with every conceivable link on it. You are better off having multiple, detailed pages on each specific aspect of your practice. The first objective of your site should be to build trust in your experience, so prospects will give you their names. You can then expose them to the full array of your services once you have that critical piece of information.

If you first attempt to expose them to all your services, you risk overwhelming them. Overload leads to delay, which leads to indecision, and the reflex of "I'll come back here later." As soon as your anonymous visitors have left your page, there is an excellent chance they will not remember to return. Even if they do remember a week or month later, the chances are not good that they'll recall your exact website address.

To sum up: It's fine to have a website that covers many aspects of your services. Just don't send all your advertising to a home page with a million links on it. You're much better off targeting that advertising to attract fewer tire-kickers and more solution-seekers. Then deliver a targeted page that addresses one of the services you offer. You'll come across as a specialist and will stand out from all the distracting, general sites. Your site can indeed become an island of professionalism and clarity in a sea of distraction when a new prospect is searching for you.

A WORD ABOUT ONLINE DIRECTORIES

Here's one big "white lie" coming from the "herd" companies selling to the majority of "Joe Architects" who finally decide to get a website. They gush about how the architect's practice will get placed on all kinds of website directory listing services where clients go to look for their future architect.

Before you buy into that, here's the little secret from the online Yellow Pages industry whose statistics show how much good a bunch of directory listings can do for you. The people from the Yellow Pages report in their traffic numbers (the number of searchers coming to the directory) that the "listing" model – the attempt to be the one stop, one source directory, like in those good old cash-cow days of the printed Yellow Pages – doesn't work on the Internet.

WHY? BECAUSE OF ONE SIX-LETTER WORD: G-O-O-G-L-E

If it's not working for THE Yellow Pages, it isn't working for any architectural mass herd website builder who promises results by putting your site up on a bunch of architect listing sites and most of the time mixed with a bunch of other services. Clients don't go there; they go straight to Google. You probably do, too! Really, when is the last time you used one of those listings to find some service provider?

Here's why. Customers (even you and I) are saying, "Why bother?" Instead, everyone is going to a place where all you have to do is type in something you're interested in and Google almost always finds it for you. When Google can do the work, clients aren't wasting time going to some architectural directory. The statistics show it: They just don't go there.

So search is more important than directories, and it's going to get even more important. Here are some incredible statistics from last fall on Net-Applications, which tracks metrics for all sorts of computer and Internet-related fields. At the end of 2009, it reported that Google controlled 84 percent of the online search engine market. Nielsen also reports that 82 percent of all local business searches now occur online, compared to 44 percent in 2005.

SEO, PPC AND GOOGLE MAP

For the rest of the discussion, I'll assume you have a very good website. If that isn't the case or you know that you can improve your website, then take action now and go to my website and look for the website review product I have available for you. If you're thinking about the Elite Program, it's one more reason to choose that program as a top-level solution to online and offline marketing and project acceptance.

When you type something into Google search, on the left hand side of the screen, you see a list of websites with a couple of sentences from the website.

You'll likely also get a list of "local" businesses that match the topic with a map showing the business location. (There's strategy involved with even that Google Map feature!) This list of searches, down the left hand side, is called the "naturals" since they aren't dependent on an advertisement, meaning you don't pay Google to be there.

If you search "residential architect Seattle" – and including the location is important in the search phrase for most small firms since their focus is local – you'll notice that some practices' websites show up in the Google local business listing (the map) and also come up somewhere near the top of the natural listings. While Google doesn't accept "payola" to be ranked highly in the naturals, it's a highly competitive game (even vicious in some markets) to get to those first few spots, and many companies pay a fortune to other people than Google to be listed there.

Why have one of those spots? Well, some of your potential clients are apt to start looking there first and may never go on to Page 2 of the searches before they "vote" for a particular architect for their project. In competitive markets, having one of those first few spots in the natural listings creates great amounts of jealousy among your competition since you are the one getting more clients.

WELL, THERE IS MORE TO THIS...

At the same time, Google is performing a search and reviews the relevant providers. In a split second, the AdWords text-ads from Google are sorted in real time by relevance and the pay-per-click (PPC) bid to determine placement. Those are the ads that you can find on the right side of your screen when you do a search on Google. This means that someone will pay Google every time you click on those ads.

You need to use AdWords to make sure people can find you if you are not consistently on that first page of natural listings, and if you are, you need to use this as a second weapon to ensure that people will find you. As you might guess, you need to pay Google to be listed there. But be advised, you can spend a lot of money or very little for about the same listing.

To achieve better results, you need to make sure you improve your AdWords quality score by writing effective ads with high click-through rates and producing targeted landing pages that are most relevant to the user's search that will result in higher AdWords quality scores, which enable your ad to earn a high position and convert that click into a new customer.

TURNING TARGETED CLICKS INTO CUSTOMERS

When customers in your local market search for products and services on Google, they are looking for a trusted, cost-effective solution. At the same time, Google works to automate its pay per click advertising to display the most relevant ads based upon the user's search query. When writing text-ads, it's important to include a call to action that speaks to the searcher's needs and relevant information to turn that click into a new customer.

For example, an ad headline for "Residential Architect Seattle" draws the user's interest and encourages him to click through to a landing page where you can capture a lead by:

- Ensuring alignment of your ad and landing pages messaging with the intention of the searcher
- Providing targeting call-to-action messages that highlight the advantages of an offer
- Including the keyword-theme within a creative, direct headline
- Properly segmenting your search campaign according to each service into ad-groups
- Keeping your landing pages relevant, up-to-date and featuring original, authoritative content

If you don't use those strategies (PPC, SEO, and Google Map), you will get few results from a website unless people search for your name. In other words, you won't get much out of it. For better results, you need to have at least two of those three and need to know what you are doing if you don't want to waste a lot of your money. This is not Vegas, baby; you need to be good at it, or work with someone who is!

NEXT STEPS

These are just a few of the techniques I use to guarantee that clients wanting and needing work done by a quality architect will show up in your practice instead of at a practice down the road that is far less qualified. As you might guess, this is just the tip of the iceberg.

Implement even half of the techniques that I've given you in this chapter, and you will see improvements in your website results right away. Don't forget that you now have a way to track the people who actually go to your website by getting their information from your new and unique offer and that you can market to them until they buy your services. The reason why they came to your website in the first place is because they are showing interest in your service. Don't miss this opportunity!

Let those other architects sit idly by, "wondering, wishing, hoping, and praying" that somehow or someday the Internet will work for them. Instead, you will have made the "no-brainer" decision to ensure your practice's website brings you more clients and revenue.

If you are willing to settle for a "pretty-looking" or "flashy" website that accomplishes little more than providing your name and phone number, fine. However, if you are interested in creating a site, or transforming your existing website, into an incredibly powerful and effective marketing tool, then you would greatly benefit from investigating my website review offer at my own website www.ArchitectProfits.com and watching your business grow.

(Yes, I was just "promoting" one of the services that I offer for architects since I do believe that all architect-owners will gain by using this service and also by joining any level of my Elite Architect Programs. I encourage you to do the same with all your prospect clients while you are talking with them: Always reinforce the benefits of all the services you are offering and the quality of those services from first contact with you until the project is done. You will see that you and your clients will benefit from this simple strategy.)

Now, get ready for Part II, where it gets really important to think outside your architect's hat. Why? Because there is a world out there that doesn't know the benefits of working with an architect – namely, you and your team. You will learn in this second section how your new way of thinking will benefit you and the clients you will attract.

PART II

Outside Your Architect's Hat...

CHAPTER 7

What About People Who Are Not Looking for You?

"It's easy to make a buck.
It's a lot tougher to make a difference."
Tom Brokaw

What about the people who are not thinking about you or looking to work with you since they don't know yet what they can get out of working with an architect? Should you try to get them to work with you, or should you not bother with them?

It's a well-known fact: Most architects want to make the world a better place. This might be coming from statements like the one from Claude Nicolas Ledoux, the favorite architect of Louis 15th: "There is no one on earth incapable of being saved by an architect." On the other hand, one of the biggest complaints architects made in one of our recent surveys was that they don't like the people they work with because most clients don't understand the value of good design.

But for years, most architects have been working with people coming to them, as opposed to looking for the people they want to work with. At least this is the case for those who have responded to our various surveys. In this chapter, you will find out how you can achieve the first and stop complaining about the second.

This might sound like a big a stretch, but it can be done. That is, when you work in a systemic way, planning and building the right strategies one by one and in the right order.

Let's look at the first part. How can you have a goal to change and make the world a better place when you are just working with a very small portion of that world? It is a well-known and unfortunate fact that just a small fraction of the population will at some point work with an architect. It would be in everybody's best interest to increase that number.

One of the main reasons for this small number is that many people don't know how and where to find an architect. The inevitable result is they don't work with architects. since they don't know who to work with. Another important reason is that there are so many "horror" stories about architects, real or not, that too many people don't want to work with one unless they absolutely have to.

I was recently watching a documentary on the Johnson's Headquarters building done by Frank Lloyd Wright. The final cost was four times the initial budget. Unfortunately, this is the perception too many people outside architecture have about what the outcome will be if they decide to work with an architect. This thinking is especially true when it comes to residential work, mostly done by small architecture firms.

One equally important reason is the fact that many people just don't understand the complexity involved in a project, from the concept to an actual building, and also what type of benefits they can gain by working with an architect.

My father is a great example of this. When I was a newborn, he decided that it was time to get a second home in the mountains north of Montreal. He decided that he would do it by himself: design, contracting and construction. He actually did it, even all the plans, and his construction documents were all on one sheet of 8 ½"x 11" paper.

The project, a three-story house with two fireplaces, three bathrooms and five bedrooms, was a success, and I have fond memories of all the time spent there.

I have to admit that my parents are kind of excessive in general and always go headfirst when they decide to do something, but if you ask my father if the next time he would work with an architect, even after that experience, his answer will be no. He easily did it once and would do it again. It was difficult for him to understand why I would want to go to grad school in architecture.

Of course, he was very proud that his youngest son was graduating with honors from one of the top ten schools of architecture in the United States. He now has a better understanding of why you would want to work with an architect for a major project and also for a residential one.

It is the architect's responsibility to promote his or her services to people who don't understand why they should be working with an architect and aren't thinking about it. The world and the architects will benefit — the world by getting better livable spaces, and the architects by getting the clients and the fees they deserve.

THERE'S NOTHING NEW HERE!

The very same tools and strategies that we will cover in the next several chapters are also used by various other types of licensed professionals and in many other industries. For example, smart dentists who specialize in implants and dental reconstructions (high-fee procedures) promote their services to attract patients who don't want to see a dentist (the reason they have huge problems), as opposed to people who go to a dentist regularly.

Numerous law firms advertise for clients in ways that make potential clients see how they could benefit from the attorney's help. The ads point out claims you might make after an accident, for example. After such marketing efforts, a client calls the lawyer – and at that point, the process has been structured so that the client feels lucky to have been accepted.

HOW CAN YOU DO THIS?

You can do the same by promoting your services outside your field. For some strange reason most architects work really hard at getting attention and recognition from their peers and not as hard from their future clients. It is more important to most architects to be published in the specialized architectural magazines than in the popular ones, even though most potential clients read the second publication. Think about it: You will get better results at attracting new clients by being published in a magazine that people outside your field can buy at their local store as opposed to some specialized architectural magazine that is hard to find, even for architects.

Why would you gain from promoting your services in media read by most of your future clients and those who are not yet looking for you? This is important to understand: This type of promotion will change the frame of mind of those future clients when it comes to approving your fees. If a client has ten architects to choose from, fees will be part of the equation, and too often the winner will be the "cheapest" architect. If you promote your services in a way to position yourself as the only emotional (and logical) choice for your future prospects, getting the fees you deserve won't be an issue.

THIS SOUNDS GREAT, BUT REALLY, HOW CAN I DO THIS?

There are many strategies that you can use, from very expensive all the way down to very low-cost. For the purpose of this book, we will mostly refer to one specific strategy that you can and should use to get the best and fastest results by investing the least amount of time and money. This strategy is simple: You just need to place an ad to get the clients you want.

CHAPTER 8

Direct Response Architectural Marketing 101

"Success depends on your backbone, not your wishbone."
Author unknown

Thinking of using an ad is certainly a new concept for many architects, especially solo architects and small firm owners. The idea of placing an ad in a newspaper, magazine or even with Google is really foreign to most, and it seems extravagant to have that kind of expense to promote your services. Why do it, since none of your peers is doing it?

That's actually not true: Very few are using these kinds of strategies to get new clients, but if you look carefully you will find some examples out there – such as Jeff Peterson's success story on Page 206.

What about interior designers: Why do they invest in full-page ads in magazines? And what about contractors? I think you are starting to see where I'm going with this.

First, let's look at several key concepts you need to understand if you want to attract new projects from those clients who are not looking for you yet. These concepts will make getting new business as painless as possible — *and* help you to consistently enjoy the highest success rate in your practice.

Any architect reading what follows can take this knowledge and apply it right away in their practice or revise existing strategies to get better results.

One reason the Architecture Marketing System, part of the Elite Architect Programs, was created was so that architects could have everything already completed for them, ready for use, without reinventing the wheel. This removes the need to become an expert in direct response marketing, on top of all of the other demanding aspects of being an architect in the 21st century.

Some architects are finding that it is a fairly time-consuming enterprise to stay on top of the latest architectural developments and would prefer to avoid simultaneously having to self-develop advertising, project acceptance systems, and their business skills. Other architects like the challenge of being pointed in the right direction and then doing it themselves.

Before we go any further into direct response architectural marketing, you need to take a look at an image that illustrates why you want to ensure that people can easily find you when searching for an architect. Instead of "any architect," you want them to look for you directly.

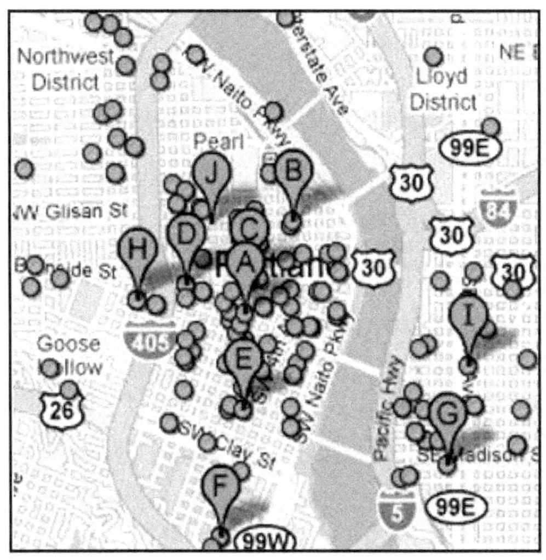

Looking for an Architect in Portland?

This is an image from Google Map when you do a search for "architect in Portland" and those dots are just a few of more than a thousand results from architects who are actually using this as a strategy to be found by prospects. Depending on where you live, there might be fewer dots, or many more.

How can you expect that all those architects will get clients from the Internet, even if over 80 percent of people now start their search there?

Not only do you need to take action to ensure that people will find you, you also need to take action to ensure that they will know what they will gain and what it will be like to work with you.

STUDY THE RIGHT KIND OF MARKETING TO GET CLOSER TO WHAT WORKS BEST

The industry that is the best at sales (project acceptance) of any kind is known as the direct response industry. You may have heard of some names from that industry and maybe have the extra time to embark on a self-study course to come up with your own systems and advertisements. If not, keep reading and find some of the information you need to get the new results that you want for your practice.

Through a considerable outlay of time, energy and money, I have specifically adapted proven direct response methods to architecture.

The foundation of the entire Architecture Marketing System was built on a number of principles, including:

- Direct response marketing techniques
- The psychology of effective customer follow-up
- Systems to manage each potential client from the first contact, through the prequalifying/screening process, and to the point where qualified clients say "yes" to you
- The identification and elimination of barriers in the sales process
- Internal administrative systems for how the team and architect interact with the potential client

Onward to the most critical direct aspects of direct response marketing that you need to grasp to get the clients you want to attract to your practice from your first ad!

DIRECT RESPONSE MARKETING – KEY FACTORS

Everything you do when promoting your services to attract new clients and those who are not looking or searching for you must be based on the solid principles of direct response marketing. (Let's abbreviate that phrase to "DRM.")

When done correctly, DRM has three key factors that make it instantly recognizable in the marketplace and explains why it works.

KEY FACTOR #1

Always send out a **problem-solution-based message.** For example: "You, Mr/Ms Prospect, have a serious problem — and it's only going to get much worse, if you don't do anything about it. But fear not: *We can fix it and provide you what you really need*, with our advanced skills and techniques. That is, provided you see us before it's too late. When you pass that point, you're toast."

The client has a specific problem: money, time, not enough space, etc. For those clients who have the problem, offer them the ideal solution. Why should you focus on a problem-solution-based message? Fear of loss is a much more powerful motivator for most of the population than possibility of gain. Not convinced? Think of how some politicians use fear to get what they want.

You might say, "All my clients come to me for their dream project." This might be true, and it's fine to stimulate both motivators; however, pushing "fear" will give you far greater result.

KEY FACTOR #2

Correct DRM has built-in ways to **measure and track results**, giving you an **ROI** (return on investment) ratio.

If you aren't tracking (or can't track) results, how do you know if that form of marketing should continue to be one where you commit resources? By tracking results, you can determine whether a particular marketing effort is performing. If not, your resources need to be moved somewhere else.

To give you a baseline to measure from, you develop a proven control ad (one shown to work to an acceptable level). You then monitor its results in a particular medium. If it doesn't live up to expectations, you know immediately you must either change the ad or change the location.

In that sense, successful direct marketing is a matter of coming up with the best ad headline and "fear of loss" message that you can, placing it where you think it will do the most good, tracking its performance, adjusting either the message or the medium, and then continuing this loop until you achieve your desired results. You can do this on your own or be part of a select group of professionals where you can exchange your experiences for faster and better results with less wasted time and money.

KEY FACTOR #3

Good DRM-based ads make an offer, if possible with a deadline, and ask for a decision. Humans like offers, and we all are motivated by deadlines. This is also referred to as putting a "call to action" in your marketing efforts. DRM will out-pull (meaning outperform on number of responses and a higher ROI) any "image" advertising that doesn't directly solve a specific problem. This has been proven over and over in testing in many different industries.

By the way, having the ability to measure what's happening is a foundational basis of DRM and most importantly allows you to stop repeating things that are not working. The example of the ad in the Tim's case study is a great example showing that it can be very small when done properly.

WHY ISN'T THERE MORE DIRECT RESPONSE MARKETING?

In fact there's a great deal of DRM out there, and you've probably responded very well to it over the years. You simply weren't aware of it, or educated enough to recognize it. Every month, we study an example of direct marketing as part of the Elite Architect's Newsletter to get better at it.

Once you understand the concepts, you'll begin to observe more and more of these ads for every conceivable product and service during your day-to-day activities. One of the clever aspects of direct response is that if you don't want or need what's being offered, you tend to not notice the ads. Only those who need the service or product (or know someone in their immediate circle of friends, coworkers, or family members who need the same) will pay much attention.

DIRECT RESPONSE IS THE FIRST STEP IN YOUR FUTURE CLIENT PREQUALIFYING PROCESS

For the architects seeking to work with clients who are not looking for them, DRM should be the first step in prequalifying a prospect and getting closer to figuring out who has the critical problem and needs the help of an architect. Direct response handles that task perfectly because it allows you to put screening steps in place to eliminate most of the unqualified clients without meeting with them or taking a phone call.

Unfortunately, prequalifying steps usually don't appeal to the graphic design artists or to most image-based copywriters in the advertising world. Or to most architects, for that matter. Why? Because screening steps can only happen with words (copy). They do not happen simply by showing a beautiful person in front of a beautiful new project. In other words, it takes more work, skill and a sequential thought process behind the ad and the systems inside the practice.

HERE'S MORE ON IMAGE MARKETING

Graphic artists like to produce ads that are visually appealing and that win awards for their design (art!). Those are what govern their underlying aesthetic and thought process. However, needless to say, great art doesn't necessarily make for great new project attraction.

The advertising industry really likes "art" and "image/feel good" style advertising for another very big reason – *it isn't measurable* and therefore the results and the advertising exec's job, income, prestige, etc., are safe from scrutiny. Advertising awards are given to the best-looking ad, not the one that produced the best results for the intended promotion.

If you read the business pages, you will notice that big corporations are constantly shifting from one large ad agency to another. There can be only one reason for this: The cost of the agencies' services outweighs the results they deliver. In trying to "out-art" one another, they have drifted away from the measurable principles of direct response. In a triumph of packaging over content, many of their beautiful ads have yielded abysmal sales results.

SOME EXAMPLES OF DRM INDUSTRIES

The two industries that understand these techniques the best are the catalog sales and direct mail industries, both of which employ the same DRM principles contained throughout the Elite Architect Program and Systems. (By the way, catalog sales is *the* biggest grossing business in the world. Why do you think you find your mailbox stuffed with catalogs every week? Because they WORK!)

I know what you're thinking: "How can a catalog successfully sell big-ticket items as expensive as what we do in architecture? Give me proof."

Consider this: Just a few years ago during a holiday season, by catalog sales ONLY, Neiman Marcus sold out of fifty "special edition" $140,000 BMW 6 series coupes listed in its catalog in 90 seconds! The ad was great, with a specific time when those BMWs would go on sale, and poof, they were gone. And that was without the people even seeing the actual cars. That's $77K per second! Does direct response work? And does it work for big-ticket items? End of discussion.

It's no surprise that the highest-paid copywriters in the world ALL work in DRM. The above facts explain why we combed these industries for strategies to get clients needing new projects to respond and say, "Yes, Mr. Architect, I've got the problem you have the answer for."

A quick and easy way to cut significant time off the development of a direct response ad for your practice is to edit and adapt a successful ad from another industry for your practice. Successful ads can be found in major national publications that run consistently week after week and month after month.

DIRECT RESPONSE MARKETING – THE BASICS

HEADLINES

The headline of any ad or marketing piece is the most important part of the ad. Every sales piece needs a headline, whether it's a print ad, postcard, mailer, newsletter, radio ad, TV ad, website page, AdWord, etc.

You'd be amazed at how many advertisers (architects especially) ignore or don't even know this crucial requirement and yet spend fortunes on marketing without realizing this critical concept has been left out. And no, one or two "meaningful" words don't make it. I'm telling you, the word "balance" or "value" can mean a lot of different things to a lot of different people. It is in your best interest to be sure that your message is clear, straight to the point, *and* meaningful.

Pay attention to ads and commercials in newspapers, magazines, TV and radio. Surf the Net looking at marketing, and you'll be amazed at how most don't have any sort of headline. Chances are if you don't see or hear a headline, you have found a marketing effort adrift without a rudder in the feel-good land of "image" marketing.

Feel-good "image" advertising is fine for big corporations like McDonald's or Coca-Cola. They can waste tons of money promoting a "feeling" toward their brand name – *but you and I can't.*

"GET MORE PROJECTS WITH THESE FIVE PROVEN HEADLINES"

In marketing, your first impression – your headline – can lead to sales success or failure. As we saw in Chapter 6 for your website, this first impression needs to be good and picked up in the blink of an eye.

It's important to realize that headlines work best when they appeal to your reader's interests, not yours. And not only can they grab attention, they can also make your message easy to read, convey your main selling points, and lead your customer to a sale – or not.

Over the years copywriting pros have used several headline formulas that always work well.

HERE ARE MY BEST FIVE:

1. The Question: "Home remodel? Not sure if it's the right time and where to start?"

A question headline automatically gets your readers involved in your message, because they answer it in their minds. Many people will read further into your letter, ad, or website copy just to find out what answer or solution you provide. Again, make sure the question focuses on the reader's interest, not yours.

A **bad example** would be, "Do you know what new project we've done this year?" (Sorry, no one cares as much as you do!)

2. The How-To: "How to get an award winning project and save on your investment."

How-to headlines work very well, because people love information that shows them how to do something. (Thousands of book titles begin with "How to....") Think of the **benefits** your services offer, and then try creating some "how to" headlines.

3. The Testimonial: "Jane Smith's architect is pure magic. We finally live in our dream home, on time and on budget!"

Why not let your clients do the selling for you? Their commendations can go a long way in convincing others to use your services. Tip: To appear credible, always include your clients' full names and the cities they live in. And also, you actually need to ask your clients for testimonials. to actually get one from them. Chances are very low that they will think to provide you with them.

4. The Command: "Boost your business today!"

Turn your most important benefit into a commanding headline, such as "Get the office you need for your expanding company" or "Ask an architect all your questions today!" or "Get your house remodel done in just 5 months." (By the way, throwing a **number** into your headline is another good tactic. And readers seem to like odd numbers as opposed to even ones.)

5. The News: "Introducing our new 'Rest-Assured' Construction Service!"

Caution: This only works if you truly have something big to announce that is of interest to readers – something that will make life or business better. Don't try to make news out of something that's not.

Once your readers know you have something they're interested in, they'll take the time to read your entire article, brochure, letter, ad, or Web page. So put some thoughts into creating headlines that entice!

In addition to the headline, you also need to give your future clients a reason "why."

REASONS WHY

As consumers, we all want to know why we should do something. The reason doesn't even have to be all that great to work. For whatever reason, we just need a reason. In your case, you need to tell your prospect why they should contact you to start working with you.

A Xerox study by Langer, Blank, and Chanowitz shows how ridiculous this concept of "reason why" really is in real life. Since then, smart folks have latched onto it and applied it to marketing and sales principles. Now you have the inside information as to what makes us all tick!

The study setting was at a self-serve copier where customers tended to form long lines. A researcher posed as one of those customers, but instead of getting in line would go straight to the front and say, "Excuse me, can I cut in line?" Tallies were kept of what happened. The scenario was repeated many times.

Would those at the front of the line let him break a cardinal tenet of civil society and go next?

They found when people ask to cut into the line to make five copies, they are successful about 60 percent of the time, no questions asked. At the baseline, people are generally polite. The actual request was also polite: "Excuse me, I have 5 pages. May I use the Xerox machine?"

When the requestors add a reasonable justification for cutting into the line ("...because I am in a hurry") the request becomes much more persuasive and compliance shoots up to 94 percent.

The part of the study that captured people's attention though, is what happens when you add "because...." paired with a meaningless justification: "Excuse me, I have 5 pages. May I use the Xerox machine *because I need to make copies?*"

Despite the circular reason, the compliance rate for the *"because I need to make copies"* request was a somewhat stunning 93 percent. Giving an empty reason was just as effective as giving a good one. Based on this, Langer and colleagues suggested that in certain conditions our consideration of the actual reason for a request may be mindless. Others have extrapolated on the finding to suggest that you don't really need to bother with the reason bit. You just need to say "because." Compliance happens.

To get the best results, give good value and be sure to give your prospect reasons to do something or not. Now that I've convinced you that direct response marketing does indeed work, let's take a closer look at architectural marketing.

CHAPTER 9
What About Architectural Marketing?

"When you are expected to exceed expectations, expect the unexpected."
Oleg Vishnepolsky

Let's take a closer look at what is currently not done right in architectural advertising and the biggest problems with what had been done.

PROBLEM #1

Most architectural advertising is, like for most other industries and other professionals, either designed by graphic designers (creating art that doesn't sell) or designed by the publication in which the advertising is running. ("Creative" departments in any given media are simply there to throw something together – usually copied from other marketing that doesn't/hasn't/won't work – and then bill you for the result.)

The creative departments and advertising reps in these media know nothing about making money from marketing. If they did, they wouldn't be working there as a rep or laying out ads. If you can't relate to what I mean by ads, let's bring it back to your firm's flyers. If you have a nice cover with barely anything on it and without a specific headline that will interest the specific people you are sending it to, you are wasting their time and your money. They won't open your flyer just because you are sending it to them if you don't give them a real reason to look at it. No, people who don't know you and didn't ask to get information from you won't open your flyer just because you like the look of it.

Here's a good example: One of my new top members sent me a flyer that his firm mailed to people who did not specifically request information. He explained that even though he really liked the look of it, the firm had gotten no projects and very few leads from it and was not sure why.

The cover was very slick, all black with a crisp red line on the edge, with the firm's logo and name and a quote, but not quite enough to be called a headline. Yes, it was very good looking, but I asked this: Why would someone who is not looking or interested in working with an architect open it? No answer. I had to be blunt: The flyer gave no reason for people to open it, and its good looks meant nothing to those people. Ouch!

PROBLEM #2

The vast majority of architectural marketing is very incestuous. This means that most architects and their advisers are copying what the majority of architects around them are already doing. Even more critical, or problematic, we who studied architecture have been trained to present our work to people that actually are architects. In other words, people who do understand what we are talking about and like what we like.

I remember my first final presentation at SCI-Arc while I was studying in Los Angeles. Michael Retondi was reviewing my project and going on and on about what he saw in it. All I could think was: I guess I meant to do all that, since that's what he's talking about. It was great: I barely had to say anything.

Unfortunately this is not the case when you present yourselves and your firm to your prospects, in your ads, your website, in your flyer, etc. Your prospects rarely have studied in our field and therefore don't understand what we have been trained to present in school. You have to make it accessible for them, not for your peers.

For architects who happen upon direct response techniques or the Elite Architect Programs, this tendency to copycat is a very good thing! Since the majority of architects are copying the ineffectual fluff that the "know-nothings" in the creative departments and media and graphic designers are already churning out or hiring designers to do the same, your competitors are constantly kept off your successful trail.

PROBLEM #3

Most of those wielding the weapons of direct response are national corporations. Architects like yourself, however, are not national but local and "micro" when it comes to small corporations. Thus, the industry as a whole doesn't get exposed to these concepts. Good for you, bad for all your peers.

WHEN DONE PROPERLY, DIRECT RESPONSE ARCHITECTURAL MARKETING LOOKS DIFFERENT FROM EVERYTHING ELSE OUT THERE.

DRM (as well as most strategies and tools in the Elite Architect Programs), if done correctly, will look different from other material out there in the architectural industry. Do not be afraid of this! In fact, celebrate it and prepare to feel quite smug knowing that when you are spending your time and money you are obtaining a result that puts more money in your bank account. You can have more time to design better projects, and ones you want: You won't have to work on just anything that comes to you.

By the way, your marketing efforts aren't meant to impress your wife, husband, brother, religious leader/spiritual adviser, buddies at the golf club, or (insert your choice here). Marketing is there to do one thing only, and that is to return clients and projects to you and your business.

DON'T FORGET THIS IMPORTANT POINT!

ARCHITECT, STOP LOOKING AT WHAT EVERYONE ELSE IS DOING TO DECIDE ON YOUR MARKETING

Let's consider a few more things on marketing inbreeding, since it is such an important topic. There is a lot of resistance among architects to being different from their peers. I hear this all the time: "Yeah, but this is what everybody else is doing, so this is what I need to do if I want to 'compete' with them." This is just a bunch of baloney! Unless you want to be like everyone else, and that means that you want to be average, you need to step outside your architect box and set yourself apart from the masses to actually stop competing with them!

What's the universal whining complaint that many architects make? "No one taught us business or marketing in architectural school!"

Sure, architectural schools could extend their programs by one or two years and tack on an MBA at the end, piling up more debt on students' backs. Instead, we all learned that it was part of the profession to make no money, that you have to be in this field for your passion of it, and somehow we became content with this reality.

While this understanding of why architecture schools can't be expected to be good at teaching business and marketing may make some of you feel better philosophically, it's time to stop blaming your schools for any lack of marketing and business skills. We still have to deal with the consequences of not having those skills. Let's get back to the real world.

ONE LAST WORD ABOUT IMITATION

The adage says, "Imitation is the highest form of flattery." Let's rewrite that for our purpose. "Imitation of successful and proven marketing is the highest form of flattery." If you are going to imitate, only imitate things that are shown to work and be highly effective.

Unfortunately, some architects can't bear the thought that very effective strategies will look substantially different from what most other architects around them are doing, even though "standing out" to get projects will bring them more income.

The bottom line: To have the greater success in promoting your services to attract more projects in your practice, you have to extract yourself from the "inbred" marketing circle before permanent genetic damage occurs to your thinking.

Okay, so you now understand that you need to develop your direct response (problem-solution) messages and advertising, and you have some guidelines to start putting in place your project acceptance process. Along with all of that, you will fine-tune your administrative systems, meaning that you and your team will know what to do and will know how to deal with the phone correctly. Now what?

To find enough clients with the projects you are seeking, **you HAVE to use mass media.**

WHY MASS MEDIA?

Several times we've discussed how few people will contact an architect on their own. If you do nothing, most people in the population won't look or think of working with an architect, especially for residential work.

Taking that into account, you must find a large enough pool of potential clients with the right problems, needs and dreams so that statistically, following screening and elimination of the "no" answers, you have enough potential projects for all of this to make economic and rational sense.

Mass media include the traditional biggies (newsprint, magazine, radio and TV) and the nontraditional (Internet marketing; yellow pages; and direct mail, either to an internal house list or to a purchased list).

MASS MEDIA IS SIMPLY A TOOL TO HELP FIND ALL THOSE FINE "GOLDEN" NEEDLES

Here is why these clients who will understand the value of good design and of the services of an architect are like needles in haystacks. At any given time very few people in the population will seek information and then actually go through with complete construction.

Those odds are really quite lousy. The fact that most of the population doesn't think of working with an architect is one of the main reasons so many architects get frustrated during the battle with their peers for clients who appreciate design and therefore their services. Most wind up disappointed and poorer while flailing around trying to figure out how to compete with their peers for these same few projects. They too often go down the road of lowering their fees to get a project or any project.

Yet these haystack needles CAN be found. You can even go for a full box of needles when you have the right marketing in the mass media and with the right screening, administrative and project acceptance systems in place. Moreover, finding these clients is well worth it because you will have a chance to turn them into pure gold during your screening process by showing all the benefits they will gain by working with you.

See, this is one critical difference between those two types of clients. You have to respond right away and enter the race with your fellow architects when someone contacts you because they are ready now for their project. You therefore have very limited time to turn them into gold. On the other hand, you have the time you need with the people you will attract when using mass media with the screening system that you will have in place.

YOUR LOCAL MARKET AND MASS MEDIA DECISIONS

At the local level, everything makes a difference, which is why external marketing must be tweaked for your local practice area depending on the building type you want to go for. That's why there really are no cookie-cutter marketing models that make sense. Obviously, if you want to attract home-remodel clients, your message needs to be different than one you would use to attract an optometrist's tenant improvement project. It's also why you need one-on-one focus in your practice to go over the specific goals for your practice.

SMALLER MARKETS

In smaller markets, it is likely that a vacuum exists for most architectural messages. And the vacuum for those waiting to hear solutions for serious projects will be BIG. This of course works in your favor, so use it.

Smaller markets are also less fragmented (potential clients are easier to reach), which means that the three traditional media may literally dominate the market, making each of those venues a great choice. The Internet is ubiquitous and cannot be ignored in smaller markets, or in any market for that matter. Architects in small markets who get moving on the Internet sooner rather than later can grab an insurmountable lead over the competition.

It's easier to test many different strategies more cheaply in smaller markets because all the media are far less expensive than in larger areas. Of course, you still have to know how to use the various media to generate enough responses to apply your screening steps to get to those gold needles. It's a stretch from what most architects are used to dealing with, which is a phone call once in a while from a potential client. The reason most architects are not used to have a screening process is simply that there is no need for one.

MEDIUM-SIZE MARKETS

In medium-size markets, such as Portland, the best medium could be any of the big three. However, because of escalating cost, it is unlikely that you will use all three of the traditional mass media outlets. The Internet is already a big factor in this environment. You will likely wind up with a combination of two of the three traditional medias plus combinations of the nontraditional mass media.

This market requires more testing but still has many of the "vacuum" characteristics of the small market, which means you can fully test without too much risk to find the sweet spots in the media you will use.

LARGER AND LARGEST MARKETS

It's a very different world for those of you who practice in the most competitive environments in the world. These include huge metropolitan regions such as New York, Chicago, Seattle, Los Angeles, Houston, Sydney, etc.

In the larger markets, the risk goes up for making mistakes and wasting large amounts of money since you are competing with the much larger firms that can afford to lose money. That's not smart of them but still a reality. It is likely that only one form of traditional mass media will be in the budget, with the remaining mix consisting of the non-traditional forms.

Effective marketing in the right media will generate excellent results, but you have to know what to do and what not do, and you have to be far more careful about your strategies.

Internet use is the highest in larger markets, and an effective website using direct response principles needs to be on your priority list. It should hearten you to know that only a few architectural practice sites are designed in this way, again giving you a major head start in this area.

SPECIFIC MEDIA

No one medium will deliver all your projects. It will always be a combination of several forms tailored to your particular location and specific type of work in your practice.

NEWSPRINT

The good old newspaper has the least expensive cost per thousand views of all media AND it has longevity (ads can be clipped and saved, which isn't possible with broadcast ads).

Yet newsprint is a mutating and possibly dying medium. The downside is that the cost per thousand customer views is going up because of the shrinking ad revenues. The good news is that the prospects you are looking for are STILL reading the paper.

There are specific times, days, and locations in the paper that work best for newsprint with direct response marketing and for the types of clients you are seeking. Most newspapers now have their advertising kits and demographics available online. These will usually be buried at the very bottom of the home page in tiny print ("advertise with us").

The reality that they make this information hard to find shows that most newspapers prefer to play down the fact that most of their money comes from advertising – and that they need to sell more newspapers to warrant bigger ad revenues. Needless to say, this influences everything they do, the content they write, and the general "shock" appeal.

If you can't find this information on the home page, simply call the newspaper's advertising department and ask for a media kit.

GLOSSY MAGAZINES

Glossy magazines (local or not) can be a big money drainer if you don't know what you are doing, because MOST are about image versus substance.

On the other hand, intelligent, direct response style marketing can and does work in these publications. Take some time to go through magazines that people outside of architecture read and you will notice that many interior designers use this medium to get new projects. Hint here: If it works for them, it will work for you. And by the way, for those of you who do residential work, those interior designers are direct competition for your work. They indeed do full residential projects, including the architectural part of it. You can't complain about it if you do nothing to compete with it.

THE INTERNET

Twenty-five to 30 percent of your efforts should be focused on Internet strategies. However, remember the Internet is JUST another medium where all of the same direct response principles apply, because people behave the same way. Strange concept, I know!

Even though the Internet is global, pay-per-click advertising allows you to easily apply effective direct response principles right away in your local market.

Some clients are making their entire buying decision simply by viewing the practice's website – meaning they either call the firm or move on to the next one. That's reason enough to get in gear and get going with direct response based marketing.

These days, it is nonsense not to have a website and not to use the Internet as a tool to find new clients. I've said it before and will say it again: It is an expense that you cannot afford to avoid if you want to have your own practice. It's that simple. If you don't have a website yet, you need to stop reading this and go back to Chapter 6. Go to my Free Marketing Course, and act on it now!

YELLOW PAGES

The Yellow Pages is another medium that is undergoing dramatic changes year by year, and we covered some aspects of this reality in the section related to your website. Many even predict the demise of the printed Yellow Pages in the not-too-distant future. Certainly, the Internet and Google are driving nails into its coffin every day. In the meantime, with the right direct response ads, it is still a medium worthy of consideration.

In medium and small markets, the Yellow Pages are likely to continue to be a good additional venue for your marketing for perhaps two to four more years. Remember, your ad should be carefully crafted in the direct response manner so you don't waste any money and so you can measure its efficacy.

In larger markets, the cost for a substantial Yellow Page ad (one that is large enough to be effective) takes a big bite out of the resources available for all your other media and venues. So think twice before committing to this medium. By the way, when was the last time you opened the Yellow Pages book to search for something?

DIRECT MAIL

Direct mail is another highly effective way to get the clients with the type of projects you want into your practice and without spending a lot of money – if you know what you're doing, or if you have someone involved who knows what he or she is doing.

The best part of direct mail for an architectural practice is that it is the most "stealth" marketing technique possible. Few, if any, other architects are likely to see your marketing efforts via this method and thus don't have the ability to mimic or outright copy what you do that is working.

Warning: There are several "direct mail" companies that prey on business owners' lack of knowledge in this area and sell very costly full color advertisement brochures.

This high upfront cost forces the architect to put all the practice's marketing "eggs in one basket." The publication will claim it is "targeted" since it goes into every paper delivery box in specific postal codes and that you can send it out to whomever you want. Don't be fooled, this is not a targeted direct mail technique. For far less cost, you can put your specific message into the mailboxes of those far more likely to respond. Those "marketing" brochures are typically not worth the paper they are printed on since they are nearly universally free of all problem-solution project acceptance "sales" boosting messages.

In addition, nothing says that you're "just another architect" like a brochure printed by a manufacturer with your name stamped on it and with a quote that says "the client is our priority" or "we are focused on design quality." (As opposed to what? The client is your second priority and you don't care about design?)

Lastly, often these materials cost more to purchase than creating your custom message on your own printer with a different headline every time you have a new ad and in which you can update critical information like new team members, new e-mail address, etc. Could there be any better reasons to throw away those brochures and seek a different way that works more effectively?

The big problem with those brochures is that they have to be very generic so you can send them to as many people as possible since you have to order thousands of them at a time. The result is that it means nothing to everybody. Also, it is very difficult to make any changes to the brochure until you are done using all the ones that are already printed and you have paid for.

On the near horizon in direct mail is something called **"micro-niche" direct mail**. It uses data mining techniques that allow mailing list segmentation. This process has become very sophisticated in the last five years but until very recently was limited to only the largest corporations because of cost. It is finally trickling down to where even architectural practices can have access to the same sensitive information that the biggest direct mailers (credit card companies) have.

RADIO

Radio still works well in certain limited local markets. In most larger markets, however, radio has become so fragmented that the cost per listener is prohibitive and does not make economic sense from a ROI standpoint.

Satellite radio, in-car CDs, MP3s, etc., are all killing this medium. Listeners are seldom loyal and change the station far more often then they self-report. Arbitron recently released a report in which it admitted its ability to really know what radio listeners are doing (which ultimately drives what one pays for radio spots) isn't going all that well due to all of these new factors, further making radio a big gamble. Bottom line is that stations may be charging for listeners who are not really there.

If you can afford the needed number of spots, and the client demographic in your area is still primarily listening to one or two local stations (mostly smaller markets), then this media may still work well for you. Fundamentally, think of radio as a medium that must be carefully evaluated on a per market basis.

By the way, one option that still pays off big, and will continue to do so for five to ten years, is to host your own radio show or be a regular guest on a show. If you have the right personality and the time, this is a highly recommended strategy to make you the ultimate architectural expert in your local environment.

TELEVISION

The proper script can generate massive client response. That being said, screening systems are even more important since not only can the response be overwhelming but most of the response will come from clients who aren't prequalified and who you don't need or want to talk to. With this medium, an automated screening process becomes even more critical since chances are really high that many people will call at the same time; we will cover how you can do this in the next chapter. How your phones are handled both with automated screening steps and what is said on the phone post-screening will play a big part in whether TV will be a success or failure. Because of cost, the stakes are high.

You can look into sharing the cost of this type of ad with other people, like a contractor you have been working with for a long time. Or you can also find sponsors to cover the cost if you address a specific topic in your ad with which they would like to associate their name.

SOMETHING TO KEEP IN MIND WITH ALL MEDIA

Always remember: Before signing any contract with any media source, test first and sign contracts later after evaluating response. Only commit to a contract after you see results and ROI. With direct response testing, you will know if the venue will produce for your market location within a very short period, which dictates further actions and whether a contract should be signed.

Also, you need to be aware of what if permitted in your state. For example, some states have specific requirements if your firm name includes an individual not licensed in that state; in others, you have to submit proposed letterhead to the licensing board, and some require that all stationary, printed matter, title blocks, and listings of the firm contain the name of at least one licensed architect in that specific state. So be aware.

CHAPTER 10

What Happens After You Place Your Direct-Response Style Advertising?

"Whenever you see a successful business, someone once made a courageous decision."
Peter Drucker

Based on the medium, anticipated response, and your staffing, you must tailor the way potential clients respond so that you, your staff and phones aren't overwhelmed. Provide multiple means for them to get information from you (for example: prerecorded messaging, website special reports, a marketing-only phone number in the practice, a special weekend phone number, etc.). In other words, make the ways clients respond to your marketing efforts easy for them.

CONSUMER DECISION MAKING

This can and should be done in ways that allow clients to screen themselves (prequalifying) so that clients who aren't "ready" for a project aren't wasting architect or staff time. For example, you can have a phone service for as low as $10/ month with:

- a specific phone number
- a specific extension number for a specific ad
- a specific recorded screening message for that specific ad
- specific reports from the people calling

The goal is to minimize the personal time lost for you and your team through any type of screening while getting the information you want from a prospect AND giving the prospect the information needed to start turning into a gold needle. Today's overheads are far too high to talk to all the potential clients who aren't likely to go through with a project. Yes, you want 100 percent of those requesting information to enter your systems for long-term follow-up, but you want the first steps to be automated as much as possible so you aren't spending all your time on the screening.

CONSUMER DECISION MAKING AS IT APPLIES TO YOU

Here's the sequence you should expect when a consumer is deciding whether to choose you. I know it hurts to think about this, but let's deal with reality here.

STEP ONE: CONSUMER SEES/HEARS YOUR MESSAGE IN THE MARKETPLACE

You provide the message. The best route is an answer (solution) to a problem that your desired client has. This could be directly through external marketing or indirectly from a referral source you have cultivated over time, a commercial broker, project manager, general contractor, or a previous client you worked with.

STEP TWO: CONSUMER RESEARCH PHASE

The consumer checks on the validity via any or all the routes available (Internet, friends, family, etc.). As part of that research phase, you can be assured most consumers are interested in things like how long, how much, how many changes, and if they will get what they want.

STEP THREE: VALIDATION OF CHOICE

Are there any other authorities or third parties who can externally validate their choice? Think previous client endorsements, awards, books, articles, reports, etc. This is where you send them information that you want them to have so they can understand the benefits of working with an architect and decide in a logical and emotional way to work with you and only you.

STEP FOUR: ACTION

When you look at the first three steps, you can directly influence and impact these steps, whether that is with the messages, expanding your circle of influence in the market, influencing the research the prospect may encounter, and providing validation for the choice.

By providing as much validation as you can, you give the prospects overwhelming evidence – it's like "shock and awe." The best part here is the more you provide, the more you control the information they look at and the better the chances that one will turn into a gold needle you want to work with.

WHY? NEVER UNDERESTIMATE THE LAZINESS FACTOR.

Think about it: If you're given the choice of going through information provided and gathered by someone else that helps you with a decision versus doing the research to pull all the materials together on your own, which route would you prefer? For most of us and most clients, we prefer that someone else do the legwork; then we can go through the information and decide.

Thus, the information, the overwhelming evidence, that you present to the potential client is all about providing the research tools so the client doesn't have to do the work. And you keep them from getting distracted by competitors.

Architecture Marketing System materials work to influence the steps consumers are taking by providing them the information they need to fully understand all the benefits that they will gain by working with an architect. Once they take action, the next steps are the internal systems related to phone and project acceptance – meaning the sales system. This is when you will ultimately secure your place in their hearts and minds.

SPEED OF INFORMATION DELIVERY

Respond to every request for information, regardless of how it is requested, in a rapid manner. Immediately mail materials that offer solutions to the prospect's specific problem, more information, and motivate the sale. Since you are the one getting the ball rolling with your ad, you can be ready ahead of time with your response.

Some of the clients coming to you via your new and improved marketing will have put off the idea of working with an architect for a very long time. Some of them never thought about this option and finally something has happened that got them to respond. It may be that your ad stirred their emotions, or something changed dramatically since your last contact with them – architectural in nature, or not.

When clients enter your "funnel" through your automated system, you need to respond rapidly to their request for information. Something in the advertisement "clicked" with something in their brain and set those fingers dialing the phone or clicking on a website. Now that they've taken action, you need to get the solution to them ASAP. That means mailing information out Monday through Friday and the use of an auto-responder on your website.

It's very important to understand that clients can enter and exit states of readiness for starting a project in very short periods. In one week's time a client can go from saying "yes" to "no." A big bill could come in (yet again!), or the car could break down, and they postpone the project.

If the prospective client has already received your prequalifying and problem-solution marketing materials from your office, and has self-qualified and is now calling the office directly, then close the consult on the phone as quickly as possible and get the prospect into your internal project acceptance system. Remember, time is of the essence with these clients.

TYPE OF INFORMATION DELIVERED TO THOSE RESPONDING

All the materials you give to potential clients must be carefully designed to address every possible component of the problem, and the reasons that a client has responded to your problem-solution based marketing piece or ad.

The sheer volume of evidence needed for a client to wholeheartedly believe that you are "the one" architect to do the project will certainly shock you and your team. Yes, it will be more than the two folded sheets of a brochure, even if printed on both sides.

However, if you take the time and effort to develop that pile of evidence, you will be the one architect they are most likely to buy from, right now or even years down the road.

Everything that the client receives from you must be designed to shorten decision-making time, get a "vote for you," and devastate the chance of another office getting your project.

Here's the goal: When clients compare what they have received from your practice to one offering similar services, the scale should still be tipped decidedly in your favor. How can that be possible?

Fortunately, most practices are so inept at this component that it is easy to tip the scales. You do so with the "evidence" you compile on what you do, the sales message for the problems you solve, and why your way of doing things is different from anything else out there.

By the way, your materials that each potential client sees should be tailored to force self-screening based on readiness. This allows you and your team to focus on the even more critical aspects of project acceptance that happen inside the practice and on actual projects. Once the prequalified client is inside the practice, it is time for you and your team to stay focused on the sequence of events that promote project acceptance (your sales system) right from the first contact.

The prequalifying concept might still sound strange to you, especially if you have never done any proper form of marketing for your practice. Most firms jump on any new prospects calling their office since it does not happen on a regular basis, especially these days. Keep in mind that this was before you started promoting your services with the different strategies we are talking about in this book and that you will put in place in your practice.

WHY YOU NEED TO FOLLOW UP

Wait a minute, we already covered the importance of follow-up! Yes we have, and it is now time to follow up on this topic since it is such an important one to easily increase results in your practice, gaining the projects and clients you want to work with.

Most practices that do any kind of marketing just let it drop at that – or, at the most, they contact the prospects much later when it is so late that they have to restart the process. If the client wasn't immediately ready, most firms will move on and keep hoping that they will find those that are ready. This is throwing money away.

I have the same discussion with all the new members joining the top two levels of the Elite Architect Programs. They all understand that it makes sense that you should stay in constant contact with the people who have previously contacted them by follow-up. However, none of them have a system in place to achieve this until they start working with me.

LET'S THINK ABOUT THIS ONE MORE TIME

Because of the time and money commitment it takes to undergo a full project, many clients have to plan their finances, family life, social life, business schedule, etc., around when they will undertake construction projects.

The bottom line is that there are many clients who aren't ready right now but will be ready in the future. Nevertheless, they contacted your practice as part of their information gathering process. Do you want to throw away a future project that you paid for with your time and from your marketing efforts just because they weren't ready in that very short time frame? Absolutely not! Yet that is what the majority of practices do every day.

How many times have you told yourself "what was the name of that person I met a few months ago; he would be perfect for this job…" or "what is the name of that restaurant we went to not that long ago and really liked" and just can't figure it out. It is similar when people contact you or meet you randomly in a social setting and you don't give them any sort of follow-up to remember you on a consistent and systematic basis.

Over time, your marketing system can and should create a *Holding Tank of Future Projects,* where you continue to "build a foundation" for projects from those potential clients who previously contacted your practice. Remember that if they contacted you in the past it's because they are potential clients. otherwise they would have not contacted you in the first place. If a client isn't ready right now and yet they still respond to the marketing in your system, then they go into the Holding Tank and are contacted with follow-up materials designed to push buttons about their condition until they literally "buy or die."

This is also your chance to cultivate them and turn them into gold needles. If they were not sure that you were "the one" at the time they contacted you, this is your chance to show them that you are. Most of the time, with the right strategies, those people will transform themselves into your best "followers," also known as your "herd" in the marketing world.

Remember, the amount of money they will be investing with you is huge. The more they are convinced in advance that you are the one, the easier it will be for them to work with you, since they will trust your ability to provide them the best project that they can get. All very good for you, and for them.

WHO RESPONDS IF YOU GET THE RIGHT MESSAGES OUT WITH YOUR MARKETING?

The first type you will encounter when using the right marketing strategies are those who simply didn't know where and how to find an architect. This would seem simple to anyone in this field, but the reality is that most people outside architecture just don't know where to look and upon what they should base their decision to select an architect. Since it involves a great deal of money, most people just decide not to take the risk of finding the wrong one.

The second type who respond to this type of marketing are often the ones who have put things off so long that their problems are now advanced. One of the people who called Tim (whom you will meet later in this book, if you haven't skipped ahead) waited ten years before calling an architect, and she told him she decided to call him that day because she found the ad "very intriguing" and he might be able to help her with her project. Ten years!

BOTH OF THESE TYPES NEVER THOUGHT OF WORKING WITH YOU.

Once their problems become larger than their willingness or ability to adapt, they become ready and act even though problems and inconveniences may have been longstanding. This can be that the office is too small or that the roof is leaking for the third winter in a row, or that more kids (or grandkids) mean the house needs to be bigger. It could be that sales are up, the company's image and direction have long since changed, and it is time to open a new store because the current one does not reflect what the company has become.

Whatever their need, prospects see your marketing piece, direct mail or ad, in a newspaper for example, and they decide to finally take their first step in your direction to get more information from you and what you can do for them. Many factors may be motivating them. It is often just as likely that a non-architectural reason. A spouse or associate may have said it is time to take action. Maybe it's a divorce, or a significant birthday, or an imminent retirement.

Okay, now that you've gone to all this trouble to research direct response techniques and strategies, developed your ads, put together a thick "overwhelming" pack of client self-screening materials, tweaked all of your project acceptance and administrative systems, let's take a peek at an overview of the whole process.

THE CHAIN OF EVENTS SUMMARIZED

1. The client with the specific problem or need is motivated: Something changes and they become "ready." A "tipping point" with something related to their problem, wants, needs, or life stage has finally occurred, if only for a brief moment.

2. The client sees your problem-solution direct response ad. It resonates with the problem-motivation, and the client qualifies himself with materials you send and the message from you.

3. The client makes an appointment, and meets with you for the first time.

4. The client then goes through your project acceptance process starting with a sequence of events from consultation to the actual project presentation, and beyond.

5. Finally, you get to the group of clients who say "yes" to working with you and only you!

CHAPTER 11

No Systems = Disappointed Architects

"The lack of external marketing systems ... is the primary reason very highly trained architects sit on all those advanced skills without ever fully applying them for client's benefit."
Christian Hogue

Systems are nothing more than step-by-step actions that lead to a desired end result. Externally, you need to use systems to deliver the prospect to your internal management and sales systems. Internally, you need to use systems to eliminate as many of the "unlikelies" as possible while placing the "likelies" on a well-planned project acceptance (sales system) pathway – the pathway to "Yes."

EXTERNAL RESPONSE SYSTEMS

You must dictate how clients get in touch with you in order to control their access to your information, deal with response volume, efficiently screen for readiness, and control the sales process as much as you can. Your aim is to tilt it in favor of clients completing their needed projects.

For example, you can have a small ad about house remodeling that explains that they can either contact you via a specific phone line (they don't need to know this part) in which you have a specific recorded message about the benefits of working with you for the house remodel, or via your website, where you can offer a "report" with specific information that you want them to look at. All this exact information is based on that specific ad.

YOU MAKE THE WAY THAT PROSPECTS RESPOND TO YOUR MARKETING EASY FOR THEM AND FOR YOU

Whatever type of external marketing you put in place, be it newsprint, Internet, radio, Google Ads, direct mail, etc., you must tailor the way the potential client responds to the solution you are offering so that you, your team and phones aren't overwhelmed and you are ready with exactly what needs to be done and said.

SCREENING SYSTEMS

We established that the total number of people who will never be in contact with an architect is enormous, and it is in your best interest to act on this reality. Now, let's refine it and look at the economics at a more understandable level. With the right message out in the marketplace, hundreds of potential clients with the problems that you as an architect with advanced training (and you do have advanced training compared to your clients) wish to help will "hold up their hands" to tell you they want you to start talking to them about a solution.

To avoid wasting your time with non-starters, you need to have in place a *screening system* that will weed out all those Type 1 and Type 2 clients we talked about in Chapter 2. Why would you take some of your time to personally do it when there are screening systems available to you that are much more cost-effective than giving your time "for free" to those clients who won't work with you?

The screening system you want to develop should automatically send those who inquire a selection of printed materials explaining the benefits of working with an architect (you), and the approximate costs. When this system has done its job of sorting and sifting, only a small portion of the "potential" clients will actually take some of your time (money) and not go on with an actual project.

This is exactly what you want. You want those who can't or won't go through with a real project to select themselves out without your intervention, and without your paying overhead (your own time or your team's) to help them make this decision.

So to summarize: When you market to attract people who were not looking or thinking of working with you, you first want to eliminate the respondents who are just tire-kickers and time-wasters. With your filtering system, this can and should be done automatically. Does that make the whole thing a fruitless exercise? Far from it – you just won the lottery. You now have access to a new pool of good prospects, and none of your peers will have access to this pool to compete with you.

The actual number of projects you can handle depends on how many hours a week you want to work and how many people you want in your team. I'm sure you are starting to see both economic and time-efficiency reasons to see those clients who are not looking for you.

Once you've placed an ad, a large percent of the activity that follows is using systems to prequalify those who respond.

SCREENING FOR READINESS, OR PREQUALIFYING

What exactly do I mean by this? Well, it's simply a matter of finding out whether those who respond to your marketing really are good candidates for the services you're offering. This includes ascertaining whether they have the necessary access to funds, and whether they're genuinely ready to go ahead, or just tire-kicking.

This is one of the great aspects of doing this type of marketing: You have the advantage. That's very different than when a prospect is contacting you and many of your peers to see what they can pull out of you compared with your peers.

Can we ever eliminate 100 percent of the clients who aren't ready for construction? Of course not, but with the right screening system, it's possible to eliminate most of them.

So what IS the right screening system? For example, does the architect take the calls, or do we leave it to the staff to handle them? The answer is no ... and no!

No one can judge a person's intentions based on how he or she sounds on the phone, or even what the person looks like when you meet – especially when you live in a city like Seattle! And with the overhead in an architectural practice, you cannot afford to let your staff be the primary screening tool.

The first step of this process is for potential clients to be routed through a special phone number where they hear a recorded message and leave their mailing address to receive further information. There is the option for those clients who don't want to leave their information to call the office directly. However, they have had to listen to a message that helps them decide if they really should call the office live, or simply leave that voice mail.

You might be thinking that you never had that problem with the phone: "My staff (or I) can easily answer all the calls." Yes that was when you were not doing any specific direct response marketing. The idea here is not that you will not be able to answer all the calls, it's that you don't have to answer all the calls yourself to provide information at this first step of your screening process. Remember, time is not free and you have to pay for that time regardless if you are making money with it.

In any case, you will still need a specific message for after-hours and weekends, and therefore need to have a specific line for those ads – that is, unless you enjoy working all nights of the week and weekends.

The next screening step is by way of the packet of information that you deliver to the clients. Again, a nice brochure (flyer) is not enough, even though you spent lots of money for it. You want this packet to do a number of things for you:

- Set you up as the architect most qualified to see them for their needs and problems.
- Answer almost any question they may have (in layman's terms).
- Further prequalify the clients by letting them know before the first meeting the cost range for the type of project they are considering.

Clients who have no way to obtain the funds or the intention to invest the time and money it takes for a new project thus determine on their own, without your help and your time or your team's time, that they shouldn't be calling you directly. Clients self-select themselves – a novel concept! That's especially important in times when most architects are really hungry and willing to grab anything that passes in front of them.

WHAT INFORMATION DO YOU DELIVER?

The materials you send to the large volume of clients who respond should be carefully designed to address every possible component of the architectural problem they responded to in your marketing piece, ad, or website.

And again, it's much easier to have different packages ready to go and ready to be printed from your own office, based on the medium that attracted the prospect. That's better than a nice brochure. This is probably very different from what most architects are doing around you. But the "unpolished" look of the "non-brochure" package that you will send will actually work in your favor. This more "casual" look does not scream "I want your money!" the way a fancy brochure will. People do respond in a positive way to this kind of information. Just make sure that all the material you are sending to your prospects is consistent and professional. All this can easily be done on your printer and placed in a folder.

Despite this large volume of material, those clients who are most likely to "buy" will read it all from front to back. What's more, they will have read a great amount of the information you want to share with them and have their decisions made before they've even met you, which is an even bigger plus for putting together the right materials.

Not only does the right package screen extremely well, but it p*romotes project acceptance* by giving them all the information and facts they need to really understand what type of benefits they can get from working with an architect – without taking up any of your valuable time.

The materials they receive from you must also be designed to shorten the decision-making time, keep them "voting for you," and hopefully eliminate the chance of another office getting your project if the prospect decides to look at more than just you.

You can achieve this by incorporating "educational information" into the package that you will send your prospects. You need to understand what the uses of education are by keeping in mind these three words: appreciate, provoke and separate.

You need to educate to elevate your clients' appreciation of what you do and who you are. It is to help clients understand what needs to be done and why – and how it benefits them.

You also need to inform your prospect to provoke thinking and to invoke fear of the consequences of not moving forward. What are the implications if they do not do the needed project? Remember, fear of loss is almost always a stronger motivator than the possibility of gain.

Finally, you need to explain to separate yourself from every other provider and solution. Help your clients see your unique value. Help your clients feel special when you are working with them. Educate to eliminate any other solution to their problems other than you and your unique services.

When clients compare what they have received from two practices, the scale should be decidedly tipped in your direction in all possible ways. Refer to the phone section to be sure you capture their information on their first call so you can send them your package. Very few of your competitors will do this.

Another benefit from this is that many people these days are afraid to commit themselves to working with a new person and often hesitage to call for fear of getting "sold" on something they don't really want. You are giving them an easy baby step for a working relationship with you.

AFTER THE SCREENING

Okay, potential clients have answered an ad, received information to prequalify their readiness for a new project, and now suddenly they are calling your office to further test the waters. Once you get good at this, and because you've kept in touch with them with subsequent messages addressing their problem, they are now ready. Others will have received your information very recently, and are calling right away. Both will have received highly motivational project acceptance messages related to how you have the best solution and are the most qualified architect in your entire region (or put country here if you prefer…) to work on the project.

If designed properly, these professional sales tools will have continued to increase the readiness of the client and planted the seeds for further action. Regardless of which category the caller is in, with the live phone call they have now taken one more step toward you.

The next most critical phase is that call, as more fully discussed in the phone section of the book. As you already know, the staff's one and only job at this point is to *close the consult and schedule the client into their appropriate spot.*

Clients getting a "free" consultation go into a pre-blocked section of free time. Keep in mind, if you are giving away free appointment times, live or by phone, make sure your team understands that those times actually cost them out of their profit sharing, and are certainly not truly "free."

In addition, clients meeting you for free need to have very restrictive rules, so you don't throw away any more money than necessary. Such rules can be, for example, a specific time in the week that works best for you, a limited amount of time that they will spend with you, a requirement to provide you information on their project before the meeting, etc. Finally, free appointments should be scheduled far enough out that more of your screening systems are working on those clients, meaning that they will have time to read the package sent to them before the free consultation.

The critical part of this phone call is that the call cycle is short and to the point. The more that is said on the phone, the more likely it is that your staff will "unclose" the appointment. Instead, your staff should keep it simple: You want to give as little info here as possible so the prospect is encouraged to come in. "Ms. Smith will be happy to go over all that with you in the consult…"

Again, it's important to understand that clients can enter and exit states of readiness for starting a project in very short and elastic periods of time. And you sure don't want the phone to be the reason for a client to decide that they should contact other firms before deciding whether to meet with you. Don't let the phone needlessly interfere with your prospects' decision to do the right thing for themselves, the people around them, and their daily happiness and welfare.

CHAPTER 12

Consultations: Eliminating the Unknown

"If you think it's expensive to hire a professional to do the job, wait until you hire an amateur."
Nathan Gilkarov

WHAT TYPE OF CONSULT?

Your external marketing has worked, your team is getting a grip on making the telephone work correctly, and now consultations with clients who have architectural problems (dreams) are flowing into the office. You can rush right in and get going on the design now, right?

Wrong! Only half the battle has been fought. If that was all that was required, you wouldn't have time to read this book because you'd be too busy working on new projects, but alas, more of your crucial systems are still necessary. When you meet with prospects for the first time, what's the best route: free consults, low-cost consults, full price only? Well, any and all of those options are best. It all depends on the client.

The trouble is that it's very difficult for your team, or you, to "sell" three different kinds of appointments over the phone. You're usually better off having the team trained to close one thing, either free or low-cost, than to immediately give them the advanced skill of trying to book and close the type of first meeting where you are fully paid for your time.

No matter what type of consultation appointment is scheduled, there needs to be an appropriate interval between the phone call and the appointment. Your written materials are still working to do more screening. There are still some clients who aren't ready to meet with you, because they haven't prequalified themselves yet.

Remember, you give them the tools they need to prequalify themselves, so that your team, and most importantly you, are released from that time-sucking activity that most practices will try to do in person, out of ignorance. Keep in mind, every time you meet with a prospect and it does end up as an unfortunate "no," it is time and money that you have wasted and that would have been better used on either another prospect or on finding the right prospect.

We mentioned "free" appointments earlier: Most often this should be limited to over the phone. We all know they aren't free, and that free appointments cost you a heck of a lot in overhead. In addition, free will drive you crazy if you aren't herding those appointments into their own blocks of time.

It could be that you don't even need to offer free consults. It really depends on things like your staff's skill, your marketplace, the local mindset, the state of the economy, and so forth. That is something that has to be discussed on a practice-by-practice basis.

In addition, with free appointments we define what the prospect will and won't get at that meeting. This means, 95 percent of the time, a non-architectural chat with the architect. Don't give away your intellectual property, all that skill and training, for nothing. That means even when you are starving for a new project.

What about low-cost consultations? When I say low-cost, that means a standard fee. The nice thing about low-cost is that now you've forced the client to help cover part of the overhead. The odds are, low-cost isn't going to cover your true overhead. If free is the equivalent of cutting a jugular, then low-cost is cutting a minor artery. You're still bleeding to death. For that reason, you define what low-cost means in the materials the clients receive from you, and what they can and cannot expect from the meeting.

The really important aspect of a low fee for that first meeting with a prospect is that you are actually starting a business relationship. The simple fact that the prospect is giving you a small amount of money, even if just a few hundred dollars, means it will make more sense to keep working with you than start the process again with someone else.

THIS IS A PRETTY BIG DEAL IN THE OVERALL SEQUENCE OF GETTING TO "YES" WITH A NEW PROSPECT.

I'm getting a lot of resistance from my new members when we cover this part of the pathway of getting to "yes" with a client, especially in these difficult times. In general they say, "Nobody charges for that first meeting with a prospect, so why would they say 'yes' to me?" An easy way to get good at asking for a fee for that first meeting is to actually offer two types of meetings, with more benefits to the low-fee consult. Explain that this first fee will be subtracted from the overall project fee. Keep in mind that it says a lot about a prospect who is not willing to pay a fee for your services from the start.

When is the last time that an attorney or an accountant met with you the first time for free? It will be easier for you to convince a prospect to pay a low fee if you believe that you do indeed deserve the fee, as much as a lawyer or accountant does.

An important thing to remember about all first meetings is that this is where the rubber meets the road. This is your chance to show your prospects that you are the architect for them. That is, if they are right for you first.

All the motivational reasons for which the clients responded to your marketing in the first place; all the solution-based messages and answers they've heard; all their interactions with your automatic screening systems; the materials and overwhelming evidence they've received from your office; and the proper use of the telephone, have all led to the day when a prospect physically meets with you, and a whole new game begins. The risks go up for everyone involved. Everything that was pure theory before now is reality for you, your team, and for the prospect, who will decide whether to proceed with you.

Your sales (project acceptance) system started much earlier than the first meeting day. But now the in-office project acceptance/sales system becomes the next critical piece of the puzzle. It needs to be carefully defined and managed, from the first meeting to project presentation and the project start day.

CHAPTER 13

That First Meeting with Your Prospect

"You can get everything in life you want if you will just help enough other people get what they want."
Zig Ziglar

The client has made it through another layer in the project acceptance system. He may have arrived there in a number of ways. Maybe it was for a free visit, or a short low-cost visit. If your team is fully trained in that modern miracle, "the telephone," the client may have arrived directly from the first phone call into the practice. All three are legitimate routes of entry.

An appropriate interval has elapsed from the phone call to the meeting appointment. This allows all of the mechanisms you've employed in your marketing system to continue letting the client prequalify himself, thus further minimizing the amount of time that gets wasted in your practice.

Is everything related to project acceptance pushed aside once we start digging into the architectural aspect of the potential project during that first meeting? By now, I think you already know the answer to this one. In fact, here's an image to keep in mind. The sales process for new projects is like the road leading out of Baghdad. It's full of potholes and landmines that you and your team must keep watching for and avoiding, until the ultimate goal of "yes" is achieved.

Keep in mind that this process is different than when you are invited by a client along with many of your peers to submit a proposal and to meet for an interview. In most cases here, you will be the only one meeting with the client.

Architecturally, you are going to gather every piece of information you may need for the development of project options. Non-architecturally, you will continue to look for barriers that may prevent the client from saying "yes." It is also your chance to go over the information you have sent previously and any additional information you have brought with you and answer all questions.

Your team must also be in the loop on what to look for and how to go about it on each phone contact with a prospect. While you'll ask architectural questions to help fine tune your thoughts about the project at hand, you also need to be asking non-architectural questions that further pull out the motivations and issues the client may raise at the project presentation that could derail things.

In addition, you are looking at numerous practical and psychological reasons that will affect the final decision for your prospect, which is to say "yes" to working with you. At that first meeting you want to do the following two things to avoid getting negative surprises when and if you indeed get to the next step with your prospect.

GIVE THE PROSPECT THE LOGICAL JUSTIFIERS

As it is physiologically impossible to make any decision only on a logical basis, especially when investing a large amount of money, employ education and specific information to serve as the justifiers for going ahead even when the clients themselves are in denial of the emotional motivators. An easy example to recognize: A new buyer of a Mercedes Benz justifies the purchase by invoking its good gas mileage! It seems silly, but it happens all the time.

FIND THE REAL MOTIVATORS

You want your prospects to say "yes" to your services. For example, they may justify it by telling themselves they will get a better resale value on their house remodel, but the real motivator is getting the biggest house on the street. The mistake you can easily make is to not find what really motivates them – in this example, the biggest house – and just talk about the benefit of the materials you will be using for their project and the impact it will have on the resale value. If you preach the functional values of green architecture that logically makes good sense, watch out. It makes good sense to you, but if they can't perceive the value with their five senses, then it is only logical that really doesn't mean much.

How do you find the real motivators from your prospect? You need to establish rapport and then using that rapport to build trust and relationship throughout the process as a basis for asking increasingly intrusive questions that eventually yield the ***Real Motivator.*** *What exactly should you be looking for?*

If you ask three different bystanders who witnessed an accident what they saw, you'll get three different answers. This is why eyewitness accounts are given limited credence in a court of law. If you've watched the movie *Vantage Point* you know what I mean by this. The movie showed the same event happening from many points of view including a tourist, a secret service agent, a terrorist and others. Each viewpoint was of the same event, yet each was also very different.

What is the truth? One would consider it to be the facts - the actual situation and event. An attorney once said the truth can be different for everyone involved in an incident or event. They are all correct. How can this be?

The truth is that truth that each person has from his viewpoint. It is the truth as seen and perceived with all five senses of each individual. This is the *truth for that individual* as seen through their eyes, memories, likes and dislikes, past, and filters of all kinds. The real motivator then is the perceived and felt actuality, dictated by the individual's past and present and expectations. It can be and usually is different for each person.

WHAT DOES THIS HAVE TO DO WITH YOUR PRACTICE? A LOT!

Finding the real motivator has a slew of applications. Understanding what it means and accepting it, just like the other laws of human nature, allows you to progress and make your way forward. It makes no sense to deny the laws of human nature.

- What is the real motivator for the client who complains about his experience with a prior architect?
- What is the real motivator for the client who says he is afraid that the project will end up way above their original budget?
- What is the real motivator for the client who is unhappy versus delighted with your services?
- What is your opportunity?

WORKING WITH THE REAL MOTIVATORS

The key to working with the real motivators, creating a winning agreement, a successful resonance with the mind of your prospect, is to find out what their real motivator is by asking questions and listening big. And I mean really listening to get to the heart of the matter. This will usually require some probing questions beyond the first answer. First answers are almost always the logical answers. If you probe deeper, you get to the real "thing". Careful, these are often barricaded behind three foot-thick mental walls.

A prospect might tell you that he decided to call your office today because it's time to work on their new home. Yes, but why today? What happened today that he or she decided to call you and not another wait another week or call another office???

ONCE FOUND – NOW WHAT?!

Work on the real motivator with tender loving care. Many people feel vulnerable when revealing what is really important to them. You need to use agreement, acknowledgement and admiration to lead them to the final step of the pathway to "yes." Find something to agree with the client's point of view. Then acknowledge his thoughts and feelings as being heard. (You can reverse the order of that if you want.) Then, finally admire them. Tell them how special it is that they shared this information. Or give a sincere compliment of another kind.

By doing this you will help your prospect feel heard, special and often eager for the next step. The fact that you listened so well can mean all the difference when it comes time for the prospect to decide to say "yes" to working with you.

Finally, you've arrived at fee time. When talking about fees, you MUST look the client directly in the eye, no matter how large the fee. If you have trouble with this, practice it with your spouse, significant other, or team. If you flinch with the fee, you're telling the client his project isn't worth it. If you look at the floor or over the client's shoulder, you're saying "I know this fee is outrageous, but..."

Look them in the eyes, and that's an order! Otherwise clients can sense your discomfort, and it gets in the way of their saying "yes." To get the fees you want and deserve out of your services (and lift your clients' enjoyment of life), YOU have to convey full confidence in yourself and your services.

Yes, there are rules and dialogues past this point, but they are beyond the scope of this book. They are discussed in detail in the Elite Architect Programs, but to summarize: Your best outcome is when the client tells you right at that first meeting that he is ready to work with you. The second one is when the client tells you he needs to review one more time all the information you provided. Whichever is the case, follow-up is extremely important.

CHAPTER 14
Project Presentation

"To start something, it's easy. To finish something it requires special efforts."
Haroon

OK, your prospect said "yes" to working with you and it is now time to present the future project. You're almost there. You've used effective external advertising, numerous clients have responded to your solution-based message and contacted your office, and predetermined screening systems have eliminated those who can't go forward with their dream projects, all without wasting tons of architect or team time.

You've also had the appropriate consultations, gathered your thoughts on the project, identified and addressed (or you have a plan to address) all the different pieces of information you have been able to gather to this point. You've used your verbal skills to make sure there will be no surprises when presenting the project.

Now you're developing project options, and preparing your summary report for the project presentation. When it comes time to prepare project options, several things may have occurred at the previous meetings with the client to help with this.

Through further discussions, the client may have defined the desired result. Or he may have told you he has a maximum amount of money in mind to spend on the project – though both conversations are in fact a rarity. The most likely scenario is one in which the client will want you to develop options within a certain amount of money.

It's like buying a car: You sort of know what you want and sort of know how much you want to spend. Most often what you end up with, though, is not the car you originally thought you'd buy, and it cost more than you wanted to spend.

When you sit down to prepare project options, you will need to fit your new client's project into your work flow, and give yourself time to make sure you aren't missing any "what if's" about the project.

For example, should you offer any options other than "the best?" Absolutely! The reality is that budget and wants come into any projects. And since some options are less than ideal, you need to determine at what point the line is drawn in the sand beyond which you are unwilling to perform a project.

Before project presentation, the project should be reviewed with the appropriate team members to continue to look for issues that may get in the way of a "yes."

If an issue is foreseeable, take the time to fix it or to address it before project presentation, if at all possible. If necessary, reschedule the meeting. It's better to eliminate another barrier than to say, "Damn the torpedoes, full speed ahead," and then find that you've blown yourself out of the water.

At project presentation, ensure that not only the client but also any and all other interested parties are there live and in person. There are ways to build this into your sales process (project acceptance system), to ensure that the person who indeed has the final say on the project is at project presentation. Look at the points of contact that make the most sense for this to occur, and get it done. You and your team will be much happier with presentations from that point forward by making sure that "I need to talk it over with X" doesn't come into play.

The presentation itself should be done using only simple terminology. Go all the way back to the specific information that the client mentioned in his or her first phone conversation. Mention the further subjective matters that the client raised at the first meeting, and of course your objective architectural findings.

Many architects confuse project presentation with project consent. These are two very different discussions. Yes, after you get to "yes" and a deposit is down and the project is going forward, then you discuss all the necessary details of what could happen, but is unlikely to occur, as part of the consent process.

Present the project options initially without fees to keep the discussion from getting fixated only on the money. That will allow the client to focus on and think about the options and results and ask clarifying questions, versus immediately shutting down the brain over the money side of things. By keeping the project cost out of the equation, you can also focus on the architectural wants the client may help clarify and his specific questions about each option.

Most architects go overboard with technical or very "artsy" jargon when presenting, which clients just don't understand. And nor, quite frankly, should they have to know what these terms mean. They're not the architect, you are.

COMPLEXITY OF DISCUSSION

FOR NEW PROJECTS, COMPLEXITY OF DISCUSSION AND LANGUAGE USED FOR ALL DISCUSSIONS AND PRESENTATIONS MUST BE SIMPLIFIED

This is critical: Everything is presented in layman's terms. This can be difficult, so think about what you are saying before meeting with the client. Studiously avoid words that most clients won't understand.

When it comes time to review project options, do NOT go into architectural details, structure, numbers, times and so on. Instead, keep the terminology limited to the result: the future project.

NEW PROJECTS COMPLEXITY MAXIM

Less complexity of discussion =

More projects accepted +

More clients benefiting from architecture

WHY SHOULD PROJECTS DISCUSSIONS BE SIMPLE?

The reality is that this new information age is overwhelming your clients, and you. Your prospects are surrounded by a myriad of choices and overwhelmed with information from everywhere. Architects who structure their sales systems and project recommendations with simplified components are seen as trusted advisers to clients struggling with information overload and confusion.

Let's take a closer look at what this really means and how this principle of simplification should be built into your system.

POPULATION INTELLIGENCE

Average intelligence is just that: "average," which is why the IQ curve is bell-shaped. The professional class typically falls around 120 on the scale. Look how few people are more intelligent than the average professional. Then look at how many are less intelligent. It's likely that whatever you and I say to each other is not going to be understood by the majority of clients. Same thing goes for project descriptions in which nobody can understand what the architect is talking about because he or she is flying way too high. When I listen to some architects I sometime wonder if they talk the same way to their prospects and clients, and if so, what those prospects and clients understand from those architects.

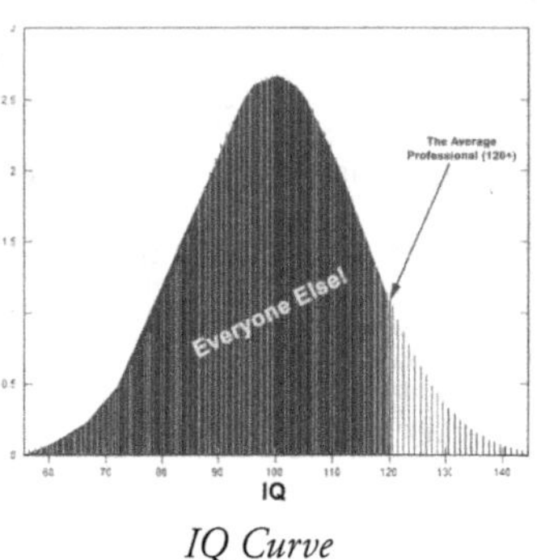

IQ Curve

If an eighth grader can't understand your message, you are in trouble. We use to say in grad school that our projects needed to be simple but not simplistic, complex but not complicated. The same goes for you when you talk with your prospects and clients; that is, if you want to be sure you are on the same page.

THE REALITY OF WEALTH AND SAVINGS

Most people would assume that all smart people have money. Guess what? It's a myth. An Ohio State 25-year longitudinal study showed no correlation between wealth, savings (assets), and intelligence. There are plenty of not very-smart people who can write much bigger checks than those holding master's degrees.

WHAT THE COMPETITION IS DOING

Most architects violate this rule and use lots of technical/artsy jargon while wondering why the client just doesn't get it. If you have a bit of extra time, go have a look at some of your peers' websites and you'll see what I mean. Let 'em! It means more clients for you!

"YES" DOESN'T HAPPEN WITHOUT UNDERSTANDING

It's already complex enough in the client's world outside architecture, and it's only going to get worse from now on. He who simplifies the world wins the gold.*

Note that none of this discussion means YOUR systems related to sales and marketing can be simplistic. Architecture is complex, and the market and sales systems for things that cost a lot of money are complex, but *discussions* with the purchaser have to be simple if you want great results.

In some cases it's the other way around: the architect language is way below what it should be, and clients get surprised by it. Be aware and be careful.

If you aren't inspecting what you are saying in your project presentations quarterly, add this into your post-presentation follow-up system.

**The Flip video camera (www.theflip.com) is an example of a simplifier winning the gold. In less than two years, this little camcorder captured 20 percent of a packed market because of its lack of features. I bought one for my parents for the holidays and they loved it because it's simple. (By the way, this is a great tool to bring with you onsite to get a clip for your clients and to collect onsite testimonials from them.)*

When the client has no further questions, but before moving into fees, you should spend some time talking about what is expected of the client as part of the project. This is one more way to help get the client on your side to make the project a success. If this is done correctly, the client will want your services even more.

After the fee for each option is presented, pause momentarily to let it sink in. The client may want to clarify which option the fee is for. Thus it's always helpful to have examples of the option you are proposing, so the client can connect the fee with what specifically he gets for that fee. Always start with the most expensive options first and go down.

Following the end of the fee discussion, the client goes home with the appropriate information from the meeting. At the same time, a return meeting is scheduled to discuss any further questions about the project and to hammer out the financials.

We have covered a lot of information so far, and now it's time to look at some success stories. You might have read a few already, or all of them. If not, let's take a look now at how others have made this system work for them.

PART III

You're Not Alone...

CHAPTER 15
Case Studies

"If you're not profitable in your practice,
you don't have a business, you have a hobby."
Author Unknown

I have no doubt that you will really enjoy reading this section because you will see that there are architects out there doing really well right now, regardless of the economy.

One aspect of their personalities that I noticed in all of the architects I interviewed is their willingness to share their experience and information with other architects. We are trained early on in school to compete against one another, and this is too often the reality of too many architects when they start their own practice. None of them in these case studies, however, were afraid to give their strategies away.

They also shared some other aspects. They all talked about their practice as a business first as opposed to the quality of their work; they all are reaching out to other people to improve their results; and most had specific goals along with a plan to reach those goals.

You will find five case studies:

1) One very young individual who is not yet an architect

2) One extremely specialized architect

3) One design-build owner

4) One of my newest members

5) One extremely "published" architect

But before we start looking at those five people, I would like for you to read what one of the most financially successful architects in the United States has to say. You can actually go to his website and watch a video of what follows…

Michael Graves:

When I was growing up, the one thing I could do well was draw. My mother on the other end started to worry a bit that all that drawing might lead me to think that I might be some sort of artist, painter, sculptor, whatever. And she made a comment at one point when I was very young that unless I was as good as Picasso or Michelangelo I would surely starve. So she suggested that I should think of using drawing in a profession, either engineering or architecture. I asked her what engineers did and she told me, and I said therefore I'm going to be an architect. She said,

"But I haven't told you what architects do." And I said, "I don't care, I'm not going to be an engineer." The next day I was on the street drawing the neighbors' houses...

My point here is not about his work as an architect and everything else that he does: That is up to you to decide if you like it or not. The critical point here is that from an early age he decided that he would be a profitable architect. And no one can argue with the fact that he indeed met this goal.

5-CENT ARCHITECTURE

The first interview is a great example that it is possible to work and have work in architecture when you are not afraid to think outside your architect's hat even when the economic conditions are difficult, and even when you have a limited amount of experience in the field.

**Picture copyright to © Mohini Patel Glanz*

There has been a lot of coverage on this young man in the paper, on the radio and even in specialized magazines like Architectural Record. He actually got a full page in this magazine – pretty good, when you know that most architects would settle just to have their name in this magazine.

You probably heard about him: John Morefield of of Architecture 5 Cents.

A little bit of background on him: He graduated from a five-year program at the University of Arizona College of Architecture Planning and Landscape Architecture in 2005; he is currently going through the exam process to be a registered architect; and he was laid off twice, from two firms, in 2008. Instead of trying to find a third job in an architecture firm in one year, he decided to bite the bullet and start his own firm.

As a smart man, he decided to apply for a "crash" business course to get a bit of background on how to run a business and had the good idea to meet with a mentor once a week. He decided to have a successful businessman as a mentor even if it meant going outside architecture, as opposed to an architect he knew.

His big "ah-ha" moment during his intensive business course was when he realized he was indeed "selling" a service, and that meant that if he wanted to have clients for his brand-new practice he would have to sell his product to people. This basic principle of business seems simple, but unfortunately most architects are not aware of or refuse to deal with this reality.

As a teenager, he worked at the Pike Place Market here in Seattle, but he was smart enough to recognize that even though he already knew the place, most people frequenting this market were tourists. Therefore, it was not a good location to start a local practice in architecture. He did more research and realized that the best place would be in a different and upcoming neighborhood. John contacted the people in charge of the farmers' market of this upcoming area and the root of the Architecture for 5 Cents was created.

In a nutshell here's what he does, for those of you who haven't read any articles about him. John has his own booth at this market with his sign, and people drop a nickel in his cup to ask him a question about their project, and he gives them a few ideas of where they can find information or tips for their future project. If they are more serious, people give him their e-mail address for a follow-up with John.

The results speak for themselves. In less than a year, he is now hiring people because of the constant flow of new projects. And this is when most architects around the country with years of experience are scratching their heads to find any projects.

His big principle: Make sure that he makes architecture more accessible to as many people as possible by keeping the process simple and making himself available to them.

Of course, once he made it outside the market and especially after he was interviewed in the Architecture Record magazine, architects started complaining about his behavior and the fact that he was not a registered architect. Some would say, "How terrible that such a young man brings the profession down to the street."

Interesting fact: Most of these complaints came from "architects" from outside the state of Washington.

On this subject I would like to say a few things to those architects. Why fight against people in your field because they are using the words "architect," "architecture," or "architectural," especially those who are opening the door of architecture to a broader range of people? (John actually does not call himself an architect when he is talking with people or in his documentation, and he is only working on residential projects for which you don't need to be a registered architect.) Instead, go against the people who are calling themselves "architect" or "senior web architect" or the like who have never studied architecture in a recognized school in the field.

I commend John for taking the risk of believing in himself in a difficult time, being successful in such a short period of time, and by giving the chance to more people to understand the benefits of working with someone who studied architecture.

Back to the important aspect of his business: "A nickel and a conversation, as simple as that," as John would say. To make things clear, he does not give buildable advice when he is on the street. Instead, he gives people direction on what they should be thinking about and what they should consider for their future project.

Basically, he opens the door to a future conversation which is an important obstacle that most people have when they think of working with an architect. The nickel is a clever strategy that he developed himself to help people make that first step to talk with someone in this field.

Is this just a coincidence? No, and he actually did the comparison with Lucy in the Peanuts comic strips. What she did was to bring something that is usually seen for the elite (psychiatry) down to the regular people for 5 cents. Most architects claim that they want to make the world a better place. It is not by working only with a small section of the population that they will reach that goal. Interesting fact: John actually proposed this strategy to a few architects while he was employed, and the idea was rejected every time.

As far as all the coverage he got in various media, he is well aware that he was the right story during the wrong economy. He understands that the impact of the "poor architect" would not have resonated so well in a good economy. The great part for him is that nine months later he is still getting calls. This is really the power of "celebrity" at its best! (NPR has run the same interview four times.)

The combination of the media coverage and his thinking outside his architect's hat put him in a position that he now has people contacting him and telling him he is the first person they thought to call. What is really critical to understand here is that, for most of his new projects, people are coming to him and nobody else. They want to work with only him, so he is not fighting with other architects on a project.

He is trying to bring the architecture to the middle class. No projects are too small for big ideas. People get the same attention from him whether for a small deck or an 8,000-square-foot house. He does understand that the $500 design fee that he quickly gets for a small project has the potential to turn into a bigger project or another client with a bigger project.

The sort of comments he gets from other architects include: "What kind of clients are you dragging out for a nickel?" On the flip side, he also receives great comments from other people such as, "You have done more in the last two weeks to educate the general public than the AIA has done in the last 20 years."

Does he see himself as a future architect? Absolutely. What about being an entrepreneur? His response was quick: "Yes I am an entrepreneur." Not only has he started his firm this year, he is also developing his "Architecture 5 Cents" association. He is well aware of the amount of work that this will mean for him to get it to the level he wants and to get the right people to represent his business model in all states.

Here is what John had to say at the end of our interview:

"When I started out, all I had was faith and an idea. I had faith that there was a need to help people with architecture. Not in a global-poverty scale but, during this recession, in a local scale. I spoke to people about the ripple effect. One conversation turns onto one job which turns into many construction jobs and so on. I needed a way to get local exposure, and the booth just seemed clear to me.

Many have told me my idea is 'genius' and revolutionary. Really? I humbly accept these compliments but in reality I'm just talking to people about their homes and what I can do to help. I tell people what sets me apart is at the end of the day – my work is not about buildings, it's about people: "It's not my portfolio, it's your home."

If I can keep doing what I'm doing and inspire more architects to follow their gut and go out to shake some hands, I will provide them all the support they need and answer all their questions. I don't consider my project of Architecture 5 Cents complete until every homeowner has been helped and every architect who has been laid off is back to work."

PUSHING YOUR PRACTICE SPECIALIZATION

For the next case study, let's look at a practice that pushes the strategy of "specialization" to a maximum. We will examine the practice of Jeff Peterson: Peterson Architects, located in Boston. Jeff's practice is specialized on rowing boathouses. Even though it is not stated this way in words on his website, you actually have to be careful to notice that he does other types of buildings.

AD used by Jeff

Was this a conscious decision to be "specialized" in this building type from the start? No, this was not a strategic decision per se, but mostly a natural evolution of his practice. He started pursuing boathouse work as a way to get the firm going when he opened it since he knew a lot about this building type. Was it random? No, it was part of the general direction of his first business plan.

As you might have guessed, Jeff had been rowing for a long time: since high school. He graduated in biology while rowing at Princeton and eventually got his master's in Architecture at the University of Virginia while coaching the rowing crew there.

It seemed natural for him to start with this building type since he had spent so much time in rowing boathouses. He already had some level of expertise compared with most architects in this area even though he was still new to the architectural world. From his first job in an office, he was already the "go-to" person for this type of project regardless of how young he was. When he decided to start his own firm in 2001, going after this type of project seemed logical.

More than this, he was also aware that there was good growth potential with this specific building type for colleges and universities because of the gender equity law. It was actually back in 1972 that this law, Title IX, was passed, but its influence evolved over time. By the 1990s, various lawsuits had caused it to be applied to athletics. This had the effect of requiring institutions to find new athletic opportunities for women, in general to balance against the men in football. Because rowing teams are large, rowing was a natural choice for adding women to the gender equity "equation" for many colleges and universities across the country.

Since he started his practice, the focus on rowing clubs has been a natural direction and an easy target for him. He never thought he would strictly specialize in this building type, but the results are there to prove that this strategy is working well for him.

In the last six years, projects have been falling into place steadily for his firm. Even more important, there has been only a slight reduction in the amount of work coming his way, even during the last couple of years of this recession. People are still contacting him because they want "him" for their project since he is known as the rowing club expert in this fairly small community.

We often say that architecture is a small world; you can just imagine how small it gets when you focus your work in such a restricted building type.

Here is where it gets better. Most of the time, people want to work with him and only him when they contact his office for the first time. They already did their homework: They called other rowing clubs to find out whom they worked with and whom they would recommend for their own project. The "interviewing" process is often extremely simplified, if at all. Jeff said he only occasionally competes with other firms for a project.

Interestingly enough, we can say that it's actually the other way around. Sometimes Jeff does get phone calls from clients working with another firm requesting his expertise. They are actually contacting him to have him review the proposed work to ensure the success of their project. Often, those calls turn out to be a new project for his firm.

For the outside architect, a rowing facility seems to be an easy game: a big box to store all those big boats and a few other rooms for classes, training, offices and locker rooms. In reality, the sequence of what is happening at a specific time can be very difficult to understand. For example, at a very early hour, when it's still dark out, many sleepy athletes gather to take several 55-foot rowing boats out of the boathouse.

The sequence of how each of those boats needs to be out of the boathouse and in the water at pretty much the same time is extremely important if you want to be sure that everything is done properly, as an accident can easily happen with those half-awake people. Not to mention that the unique dimensional requirements for shells and oars impacts both access and storage in very specific ways.

Is everything magic for Jeff? Is it simple and are projects rowing to his office in a natural flow all the time? Of course not. Jeff gets his fair share of projects but they are not all going to his firm since not everyone in this niche knows about him. Jeff actually does advertise on a regular basis for his services in the major rowing magazines. One of the key winning elements to notice here is the fact that he is so specialized that very few people would spend the time and money to advertise in any specialized rowing magazine to get new work. As a side effect of his type of ads, it is much easier for him to have an ad that responds to the "what's in it for me" reaction. Even more power to him.

Jeff's marketing efforts are not limited to these ads. He also wrote an article on the boathouse design process for the same rowing magazine and gave a presentation with a similar topic at the US Rowing national convention. In addition, he also wrote a foreword to a book called "Boathouses: Architecture at the Water's Edge." Even more, he sometimes sends promotional material to potential clients when he hears about a boathouse project if he is registered in their state.

Basically, he does everything he reasonably can to maintain his "expert" status.

His ads are very simple since they are extremely targeted. It's much easier to convey in a small ad that you are an architect specializing in boathouses than trying to say you can do any type of work for any type of client on any type of budget.

WHAT ABOUT HIS FEES?

Most of the time, he has no real discussion about the fees when talking with a potential client. It is much more of a simple question with a simple answer than a "deal breaker" question.

As we said earlier, in general his prospects have already decided that they want to work with him when they contact him. Most of the discussion with a prospective client is about the requirements for the projects and take for granted that he is the "chosen one."

Jeff noted that sometimes the clincher for him is that his firm isn't really much more expensive, if at all, than other firms he might be competing against. It also helps that his firm actually does very high quality design. Therefore clients aren't sacrificing design quality for expertise.

The most difficult aspect that he has from being so specialized is the limitation of potential work in his own area, and that he needs to convey to people outside his own state that there are ways for him to be the expert for their project even if he is not located next to them.

As you might expect, this is not a very big obstacle, especially when working in higher education, as people are most likely aware that there is no real limitation in where you can select an architect these days. Of course there are ways to go around this in your advertisement, and as a clever entrepreneur, Jeff has been able to convey this information in just a few words.

The interesting part is that Jeff was really not struggling at the time of the interview to have new projects for his practice. He also seemed to be very much removed from the realm of his peers, many of whom are struggling to get a single project, and who find themselves again and again fighting with too many other firms for each one.

Can this model be done with other "specialized" building types? Absolutely, and I will let you be the judge if it can be a strategy that could work for you. As far as Jeff Peterson is concerned, he really enjoys his practice; he is very satisfied with the type of projects he does and the clients he works with. In addition to all of this, he has the freedom to spend a great deal of time with his kids.

USING THE "DOWN ECONOMY" TO IMPLEMENT MORE STRATEGIES

For these case studies, I also wanted to explore if the people with design/build firms are using similar strategies and tools to promote their services and their projects. Here is the story of one of the most successful ones here in Seattle, referred to as the "Hot Shot" in the Northwest Home magazine.

"Hot" New Project

Anthony Maschmedt of Dwell Development started his design/build firm in 2005 at the peak of the housing industry. Because of good strategies and decisions for his business, he is now one of the six companies still open out of the 46 that existed in 2005.

Anthony always had a strong interest in housing, real estate and development. His mother is a successful interior designer in Seattle as well as a general contractor by trade; therefore he was always surrounded with this field. He started buying and selling real estate when he was really young. He was only 21 when he bought his first house and had up to eight houses at one point in his late twenties.

He then decided that it was time for a change and started working in sales and marketing for one of the biggest hair product company in the country. He had a successful career but always had an eye on the development industry.

After thirteen years of traveling all over the country for this company, he decided that it was time for another change. His mother suggested he join her and his brother to start a new design/build firm in Seattle. He decided that this would be a good opportunity for him to go back to his passion of housing and took the role of sales/marketing/land acquisition and the business side of this new company.

His first task was to put in place all the systems that he had learned during his thirteen years working for a national company and ensuring that he would make those "fit" into a business model that would work for a design/build company.

In 2005, he decided that it was time to go out on his own and start his company so he could push his ideas even further. He wanted further systems in place, with consistent and specific architectural style for all his projects, to get a better focus and better results on the end product.

The transition was really easy since it was the perfect market for an experienced person to start a design/build firm. Like he said, he would build a house and put up a sign, and it was sold in time for the next one.

When he started Dwell, his thought was, "I don't want to jump in a big pond with a lot of fishes." He made a conscious effort to stay outside of where everyone was working and search for something that would position him in a unique place.

Anthony was fully aware that this housing climate would not last forever and was already spending time looking at what other people around him where doing in an effort to be smarter about his own process. He knew that when the market is good, you can do pretty much everything "kind of good" and you could still have a successful business. But it would be a different story if the economy would change.

He contacted a local firm where he liked the type of work they were producing and decided to work with one specific designer to develop a specific architectural style for all his projects to create his own signature for his company.

That first year they quickly worked on five projects in which Dwell would purchase properties, design the projects, permit the projects, and then work with a developer for the construction aspect to limit risks during construction and for time efficiency in creating a niche within a specific neighborhood.

Anthony was very selective about where he would do his projects and decided to limit all of them to a specific area. It is important for him to have a sense of community in his projects, and to buy locally and build locally.

After that first year, Anthony and architect Julian Weber decided to partner and to create a second section of Dwell Development: Dwell Design. Both aspects of Dwell have a strong focus on green design – not because it makes it easier to sell their projects, but because they believe in it.

Anthony mentioned that it is actually the other way around with green design: It actually makes it more difficult to sell their projects to people who have not met with them first to talk about the benefits they can gain from it.

As we all know, the housing market did in fact really change, and not in a good way. In addition to the systems that he had already put in place, Anthony decided to streamline what he was doing in-house and hire people to reduce his cost on overhead and liability.

With the current economy, they now have lowered the number of projects that they work on at the same time and make sure that they are sold early in the process.

They are using this "down period" as an opportunity to work on marketing strategies, update their website, test new strategies to get more attention from potential leads, and look at how people find them to ensure they get the right information about all the different services offered.

They are also working with outside consultants in an effort to leverage their time and to learn new tools and concepts to implement in their business model. The main goal is to implement as much as possible now to keep building a sustainable business for the long term.

They are well aware that it is important to have a list of potential leads and that it is part of their continuous success, especially in this economy. This list was not just given to them; they have been working with different strategies to make this happen.

For example, they're using only one real estate agent for all their projects, and this agent is required to keep in touch with people who have contacted him about any of the Dwell projects.

They are giving tours of their new projects to this list of people and also tours of their projects under construction to educate as many people as possible on the work they do. The result is that people are aware of what they do, understand how they can benefit from it, and know the high quality of it.

When the partners have a project starting construction, they send an e-mail to these people letting them know they are welcome to visit the site – and that they are the first ones to have a chance to look at it to decide if the project is what they are looking for.

The people like it because they don't need to verify on a regular basis if Dwell has a new project that might be the one for them; they know that they will get an e-mail about it. Dwell loves it because it makes the sales process much easier.

It used to be more of a random process, based on what they were doing at a certain time. They are now looking at ways to make this process more systemized to get better results for them and their prospects.

Anthony was generous with his time, and his passion for his neighborhood was obvious: Three people greeted him during our interview at his local coffee shop.

Not only this, he also often gives tour of his projects under construction to interested architects, especially on the green design aspect. He doesn't feel the need to hide his work from his peers and from architects in general. For him, it is more about networking and sharing ideas with people in his industry.

He is not afraid to give away his secrets since he sees this as flattering when people ask him about it and believes that he can also learn from others when he does share those secrets.

He mentioned that he finds it pretty funny to see how architects are so competitive with one another. For him, there is room for everyone who does good projects.

He also mentioned that, yes, you need to be proud of the quality of your projects, but that first it is a business that you are dealing with and that any decisions that he makes have to make sense from a business standpoint first.

Anthony's big "ah-ha" during this last year is that you have to have systems in place and that self-promotion is a must: "You have to blow your horn as loud as you can and promote yourself constantly."

STARTING FROM SCRATCH

Our next case study is Tim, one of my top-level members I decided to include his story since it is a good example of what is possible to achieve when you have good systems and strategies in place in just a few months.

When he first contacted me, I remember one of the first things he told me: "I am sure I have lots to offer; my problem has always been in trying to find those to whom I represent the greatest value, but I don't know how."

When Tim made that initial contact he was new to Texas. He didn't have a website and didn't know anybody in this area since he had just moved there from California with his family.

One of his first goals was to establish and work with a business plan within the next year, and one of his biggest challenges was his lack of clarity about what he wanted his practice to focus on. Tim was coming to me with very little experience on what it means to be in business.

Most of the previous work that he enjoyed was residential, especially for the one-on-one aspect of those projects. Based on this, it was decided that he should start with a focus on this building type.

His first step was to put a website together. I helped him sort out what he should include on his website and how he could have this done cheaply and quickly by including the basic components to ensure he would get the information he needed from this tool. Tim actually did the website himself in just a few weeks.

Tim was eager to start working on a project, and he wanted to jump right in with his first ad with a specific headline for house remodeling. He did the research and decided which of the media he wanted to use. He selected one of the local newspapers for the low cost-to-reach ratio of this medium.

Tim decided to go with the San Antonio Express and after several e-mails and phone calls got the price down by 30% for one small 2x2 ad in the newspaper, in their magazine called Trend, and a banner on their website.

Once this decision was made, I helped him put this small ad together. By the way, a 2x2 ad is actually a 3.22"x2" ad: very small.

Since this was a very small ad, we decided to go with one of the strategies that is included in Architecture Marketing Systems that my members use called "PAS."

What is this? Simple: Problem-Agitation-Solution. Basically you state the problem, you agitate the problem to make sure the client knows you understand their problem, and then, you provide a solution on a silver platter. Short and sweet: This is PAS.

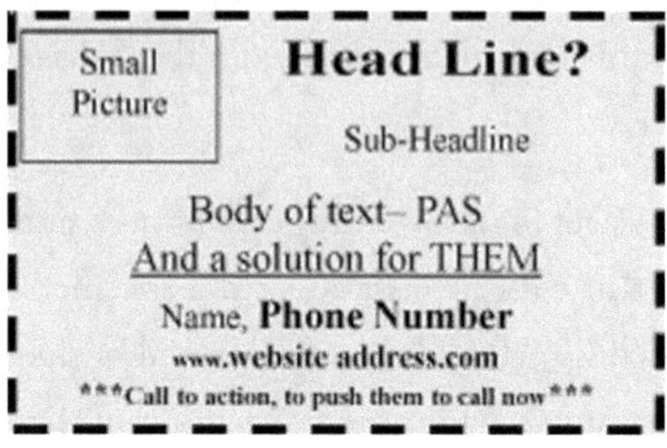

Ad used by Tim.

This is the actual size of the ad, and note that we included a small picture on the top left corner to grab people's attention. Actually, it was a small black and white drawing since when it is so small, pictures just don't look that great. It is much better to use a hard line drawing.

Then he included his name, phone number, and website. The last thing you need to notice on this ad is the bottom line, the call to action. It's a sentence that pushes the prospect to call right now as opposed to waiting and forgetting about it. There is much more to be said about each of the components of such an ad, and this is one of the topics that we consistently review in the Elite Architect Programs.

THE RESULTS: FIVE NEW PROSPECTS

Tim sent me an e-mail about two weeks after the ad ran to say that he'd just taken a fifth call generated from the ad. Let's review what they actually said when they called him.

(By the way, Tim decided to use a recording system that all calls from that ad would go through so we could talk about it later on. This is a great way to listen to what you say and take action to improve your success on this critical first step with a new prospect.)

FIRST PERSON:

"I saw your ad in the San Antonio newspaper, and I'm calling for information. We've lived in the same house for the last 30 years, we live in a good area, but in our specific area prices have not appreciated that much. We want to have an opinion on what we can do to increase the value of the house, or if we should sell as-is and build something new.

We had two different structural engineers look at the house at separate times. A portion of the ceiling is cracking more every year. We want to have an opinion to see if we need to upgrade the structure, which wall we can move and what we can do to increase the size of the kitchen per today's standards.

We have talked to a contractor before, and they don't seem to understand what is going on. We have messed around with this project for the last 10 years.

What intrigued me about your ad is that you are an architect and that we didn't think of asking one before, and I thought that you might be able to look at the original drawings and have some new information for us. So I'm not sure if this is worth your time, but I want to know if you are interested in having a look.

We don't want to work directly with a contractor; we had bad experience in the past. We have an issue that has a history, and we want to make sure we make the right decision. We're not in a pressing hurry to make a decision; we want to gather accurate information."

There were important red flags here: the prospect actually said that they have been "messing around" for the last ten years on this project, had bad experiences with contractors, and they already asked two structural engineers for their opinion and are now looking for someone else's opinion. All these are indicators that it is very hard for them to make any decision (come on, ten years!), which will translate into a long process for you, and chances are really high that it will be very hard to satisfy them since three professionals have already failed.

Tim decided not to go with this prospect.

SECOND PERSON:

I actually don't have the recording of this person since in this case, the person left a voice mail and Tim contacted the person at a later time with his own line. Tim told me that this person called because he was interested in meeting with him for a consult.

Tim was meeting with this prospect the following week.

THIRD PERSON:

"Looking for information for your ad on home-remodel."

She was actually looking for a remodel to her mobile home.

Tim told her that he was not the right person for what she needed and gave her some information on whom she should contact for her project.

FOURTH PERSON:

"I'm calling about your ad; I'm a home owner, getting my plans in order to remodel my house, if you're interested in talking with me in the near future that would be great. My house is around 2,000 square feet, I'm cleaning out my house and getting to the stage to have someone like you come to have a look – 3 bedrooms, 2 baths. The house needs a real master bedroom, new bathrooms and a new kitchen.

Your ad was a good idea; I didn't know where to look."

Tim was meeting with this prospect the following week.

FIFTH PERSON:

"Hi, I am calling about an ad you had in the paper a little while ago, I was out of town, I cut it out and now I'm back and calling you. Hardwood floor, crown molding."

Tim referred this prospect to a contractor. As you know, referrals are always good to create future work and especially a good way to introduce yourself to a contractor or to get back in touch with a contractor you already know. Obviously, it is in your best interest to do some research to find a good one before referring a prospect who came to you first.

THE CRITICAL INFORMATION THAT YOU NEED TO NOTICE

The future will tell us if Tim will get either of those two projects. I asked him what he thought of the process at this point in time. His answer was clear: This is exactly what he was looking for – a step-by-step system in which he can focus his attention on the weak steps to ensure greater success.

He was well aware that the next step depended on his ability to "sell" his services and felt confident that he would be able to improve his results over time by consistently reviewing his strategies and tools that he decided to use and to put in place.

The big points to note:

- He was not competing with any other architects
- He was able to decide from the start whom he wanted to go and meet, therefore reducing his time investment and getting the chance to focus on the right area
- The prospects were intrigued by the ad and called him as a result, even after a few weeks
- He is able to refer some of the potential projects to other professionals
- All of this for about $600. No need to say that Tim is already planning his next ad!

YOU NEED TO UNDERSTAND THAT YOU ARE IN A BUSINESS

Russell Shubin and Robin Donaldson met in the late 1980s during a project tour in which Robin was the project architect. Shortly after, Robin told Russell about a business consulting course available for young entrepreneurs and they decided to take the course together. They were both working for small successful firms at the time, and it was during this course that they started doing projects together.

By 1990 they both had started their own firm and it is that year that they decided to formalize their partnership with Shubin & Donaldson Architects, even though they were not living in the same city: Russell in Los Angeles and Robin in Santa Barbara.

Project under construction

While working full time between '85 and '89 just after graduating with a Bachelor of Architecture degree from California Polytechnic University at San Luis Obispo, Russell took and finished his architectural exams to be licensed as an architect. He also received his general contractor's license and finished an executive MBA program. Robin received his master's in architecture, graduating first in his class at Southern California Institute of Architecture (SCI-ARC).

While attending SCI-ARC he began working for Morphosis and eventually became a Project Architect for the firm.

It is significant to understand that from day one, their partnership was based on solid business decisions. They determined from the start where they wanted to go with their practice by consistently working with different business coaches throughout the years in an effort to always stay on track with their long-term direction.

These days, they actually have two sources of coaching: a consultant who works individually with them on the architectural aspects of their business, and they are part of an entrepreneur group that is forward thinking in terms of the business aspect of their firm.

It was important for them to have more than just similar design sensibility to start their partnership, which is too often the case for many partners in architecture. It was obvious to them that they would gain from this partnership since they were clearly bringing more to each other by developing two different markets while building together a single architectural language on every project, which is one of the columns of their success.

Technology made this partnering process easier over time. Russell and Robin used to drive back and forth between both cities on a weekly basis. These days, for the most part, everything is done via video-conferencing on a daily basis. Each of them leverages their own location as far as bringing new clients to the firm, while both are working on the design development of key projects. This business structure ensures that each of them is bringing their best assets to the table, especially for their "signature" projects.

During the interview, Russell referred to this process as "an active peer review," where each partner works and provide input on a project. They have developed a critical path for the development of design; each project is subject to partner review and key points in the design phases of service, construction documents, and construction administration. The process is critical to the final design since it is more than just providing general inputs for "the other office's project." Ideally, it is a productive, collaborative process, with document cameras used to enable them to work together on sketches and drawings for the design development.

Their partnership goes beyond their business goals. They understand the need of working together on all aspects of the firm to sustain the success, and they know that each has to ensure the success of his own office.

Russell explained clearly that it is important for them to understand and to implement simple business rules:

"You've got to get the work, produce the work, and get paid for the work. First, you've got to get the projects. So both people, because we're in two different cities, needed to be really good at

being able to sell – that's really what you're doing. At the end of the day, every business, if you don't sell you don't have a business.

You don't have to worry about your production, or anything else. If you don't have the sales, there's no business. So based on the fact that we're in two different cities, we both have to be more "all-around." You've got to be able to sell, you've got to be able to design, and you've got to be able to understand what's going on in terms of running projects from the office. You can't just say, "One guy does one thing and one guy does another."

Based on their business background, someone would think that they would have focused their practice on production projects as opposed to a boutique design firm. Or that they could have decided to try to do both, but it was clear to them early on in their careers that, as Russell says it himself so well: "It's hard to be all things to all people; you can't be Gensler and Shubin & Donaldson at the same time."

They actually don't do any projects that are strictly production but rather focus their efforts on high-quality production on high-design projects. They made the decision early on not to do any production projects mainly because they realized that those are not where the best fees are for their business model, especially since they knew they didn't want to be a large firm. Russell noted that he found early on through his research that typically firms that are doing high design **are most profitable.**

Who would blame them to have decided to strive for those projects and to keep their practice lean to avoid dealing with high overhead and a large number of employees, especially these days? It is simple to recognize that the reason they understood this from the start was that they had a mentor who was there when they started their practice to advise them on which direction would be more suited for their qualities, goals and desires as opposed to jumping in and hoping for the best.

From their early days, their strategy was to start their practice with a strong focus on one single project type, residential work, and then as time would go by, to branch out to other project types that would be in line with their area of expertise. It was therefore a natural evolution for their practice to start with residential architecture, to interior spaces for commercial, then **multi-family/ mixed-use** projects and now to hospitality.

MARKETING STRATEGIES TO GET THEIR HANDS ON HIGH-PROFILE PROJECTS

Their first strategy is to have a publicist on board to ensure that their work is "out there." But there are several distinctions of what is important in their minds when they say "out there." One important aspect of getting their name and work out in trade magazines is to help get better employees. But for them, it's more critical to get their name and work published in as many non-trade magazines as possible since they are fully aware that this is where their potential clients for the most part will be looking for a potential architect. In addition to the various publications, they also submit their work for awards on a regular basis to be known in the community.

The last piece toward making their work available to as many people as possible is a monograph that they are working on, which will includes a forward section from Tom Mayne. This new book was scheduled to be released in the spring of 2010 for a worldwide distribution, and they expect it to be instrumental in the next phase of the expansion of their practice.

They also stay in constant contact with different brokers: commercial and residential brokers. They also spend time meeting with developers and are active in various organizations. All of this constant work is in place to stay in people's minds when a new project comes around.

As far as regular ads in magazines, in general they don't need to use this marketing tool since they already have a large amount of coverage in those for free with all the articles that are published about them. It is important to note that they have used ads in the past in trade magazines while they were working on establishing themselves in a new sector. Athough they don't spend money on ads per se, they instead invest money in working with a publicist.

THEIR SYSTEMS

One of the business realities that Russell and Robin realized very early on in their partnership is the fact that since they are located in two different cities, they needed to have a specific time to talk with each other on a weekly basis as opposed to calling and interrupting each other's work flow whenever they wanted to talk about a specific topic. They have had these weekly phone meetings for the last twenty years.

This critical weekly call usually runs for about 90 minutes, and one of the topics that they address is their finances. For example, they work with a one-page spreadsheet to cover their A/R, cash account, the latest financial profit and loss statement for the previous week, monthly updates, etc.

Another topic that they review during this call is the results of their marketing efforts. They are using an integrated database system in which they track and make a distinction between new leads, the ones who moved on to a "qualified prospect," the ones who received a quote from them, and finally the ones who got booked for a real project. They go through each grouping name by name to ensure that they didn't forget about any of their follow-up steps with any of those prospects. For example, they may cover whether they have sent a specific postcard to a specific lead, whether they have called a person back to verify if they received the requested information, etc.

They also go through the names of all the different people they have recently met, whom they need to meet, and whom they need to contact.

AND YES, THIS IS EVERY WEEK.

They also have additional tracking systems in place to ensure the success of their business. For example, they have a system to track their current work in progress, called WIP. This system is in place to track every job and the work of every team member working on each of those projects, and also to break out the fee that is going toward each job to follow and verify how they're doing each week. This WIP is a weapon in place to ensure that they are hitting billing targets each month as opposed to just looking at the deadline directly ahead of them. Ultimately, this is in place to ensure that they stay at a certain profit range for each project each month.

THREE CRITERIA FOR ACCEPTING A NEW PROJECT

I have to say that I was very pleased when Russell starting talking about their process for accepting a new project in their firm, even in today's economy. For each project coming to them, they have to review it to make sure it meets at least two of their three basic criteria:

1. What kind of job is it? Is it going to forward their practice?

2. What's the fee? Is this a really good fee or is this a lean fee?

3. What's the client like? Is this going to be a low or high maintenance client?

Clearly, the goal is that all projects going forward meet all three criteria, but it is not always the case. They then need to decide if there are at least two strong criteria present to say "yes" to a project. For example, if it's going to be a really great project but with a difficult client and inadequate fee, then the answer is, "No, not doing it."

Why not take all projects coming their way? Russell said that they both strongly agree that it is much better for them to use their time, energy and money somewhere more productive. It is more effective to find a better project than to work on a project that does not meet their criteria.

WHERE DO MOST OF THEIR PROJECTS COME FROM?

Russell and Robin are well aware that on the residential front these days most people start their research online especially for the type of work they do: contemporary and/ or modern residential architecture. Like most architectural firms, their work used to come mostly from referrals, but that is no longer true.

In response to this new reality, they have optimized their website and are now using strategies like AdWords to attract as many people to their firm as possible.

On the commercial and hospitality sides of their practice, a lot of their projects come through commercial brokers and project managers. As we covered earlier, Russell and Robin actively keep in touch with those people and keep track of their actions in a database that they review on a weekly basis.

HOW DO THEY GET THEIR PROJECTS?

One of the first strategies that Russell mentioned about how they go about getting their projects was that they intentionally make sure that they come across as very accessible to all people on their website and their soon-to-be released monograph, as opposed to being out of reach by the way they articulate themselves.

They also make a significant effort of trying to understand the prospective client. They don't show any work for as long as they can when they first meet with a prospect, and the same is true about the specifics of their practice. First they make certain that the prospect tells them as much as they possibly can about themselves: who they are, where they're going, what are their concerns, what is it that's important to them in selecting an architect, etc.

This is to ensure that when they do present their portfolio and talk about their firm, it is within the context of the client's world. Robin and Russell can therefore change their language based on the concerns, goals and aspirations of the prospect's project.

This process of "collecting information about a prospect" starts when a person calls their office for the first time. The first thing that they want to know is why the person called them. They realize that if a person says that they "saw the company's work and want to work with them," it is a completely different game than if a person says that they "heard about the company and are thinking of working with an architect."

They really go to extensive efforts to understand what matters to their prospects in an effort to be able to present what the client wants in this working collaboration. Russell and Robin make an effort to talk inside their prospect's world-view: What is it that the prospect is looking for as opposed to what Russell and Robin think they want.

Russell mentioned that one of their best questions when talking with a prospect is, "What are your concerns in doing this project?" He also added that they are fully aware that it really pays better to be more concerned about what matters to their clients as opposed to what matters to them.

There are a lot of great architects in California, and Russell strongly believes that the main reason that they get the projects they want and that they are still successful in this economy is that they are proficient at showing prospects they are thinking in their best interest.

He also believes that the best way to achieve this is when you really try to understand what the prospect's concerns are by simply asking as many questions as you can.

Obviously they also need to express that they know what they are doing and that they will be producing a project of the highest quality. But ultimately, it comes down to how "relatable" they are and that they "get" the prospect's needs.

THEIR SUCCESS IS FOUNDED ON SOLID GROUND

At the end of this interview, it was obvious that Russell and Robin are not trying to please everyone, that they have a very strong sense of what they want to do, what they are willing to do, what they don't want to do – and that they are not willing to make compromises for a project if they don't believe in its potential, because at the end of the day, nobody will benefit from it.

Their success is the result of many years of consistently working in and on their practice, by implementing strategies and systems that they went out of their way to learn and that they are still consciously seeking to improve on a weekly basis. They are extremely talented as architects and extremely smart as business people.

Russell ended the interview by saying; "You can't be all things to all people; it's too hard to do."

Chapter 16
What Is Your Comfort Zone?

"You've come a long way, baby!"
The Philip Morris Company

Pssst. Guess what? You and I know something that no one else knows. It's pretty weird isn't it? Architects are the most perfect humans on God's green earth, right? Crazy that everyone else can't seem to figure this out. Come on, people out there, isn't it obvious? Someone get the president or head of the United Nations to make a global proclamation. Geez, Louis.

Okay, the spoof is over. You do have pretty high standards wired into your professional genes. And thank heavens for the clients' sake that you have this built in genetically, or that it was implanted or beaten into you by educational faculty.

That wiring keeps your clients a whole lot safer and gives them better results, better projects, more bang for their buck, etc. How do I know this?

Well, no matter how many times you develop options for them, do multiple coordination, go over a plan for the tenth time, if and when you encounter "unexpected discoveries" or other complicating factors, your stress level and blood pressure go up. Instead of saying, "Too bad, I'm out of here," you go into "Mr. Perfect" mode to fix things.

THE ILLOGIC OF PERFECT THINKING

Now while this is great for the public and goes unrecognized for the most part, this trait in you as an architect IS a sharp double-edged sword. There is some illogic about perfect thinking that can bite you on the derrière (excuse my French!). There are plenty of times the standard should be "Mr. Acceptable."

Yes, there are times where you create unneeded stress on yourself when you need to deem that "nearly perfect" is a very acceptable result. Non-architecturally is where Perfect Thinking can make a bigger welt on the hiney. Here's how. When you start anything new, especially when acquiring new capabilities like say putting into place a process to achieve better project acceptance, you can't be perfect and that's really okay.

In case you haven't noticed, that's a lot of what this book is about: providing the processes that give your practice non-architectural capabilities so you can harvest architectural opportunities.

Too many times with new non-architectural systems, architects will want something to be perfect before they even try it, and that's just not possible. So, guess what, no actual progress in a forward direction happens if that type of thinking is applied to the non-architectural capabilities.

Keep in mind: Everything you really want is usually outside your comfort zone.

If that doesn't make sense, here's an example that you can relate to. Remember that first model, that first exterior elevation, that first cross-section, the first site plan you did? For most of us, that sure wasn't perfect. (Remember, they didn't gas us at the beginning during freshman year; they waited since, after all, there was a risk of asphyxiation and they didn't want to lose the tuition!) It took continued action (forced upon us by grades/fear/rewards) to make those actions turn into a repeatable process that you could do in your sleep. Right?

So, guess what? Instituting new actions, putting into place systems, delegating to your key person, obtaining capabilities (especially the non-architectural ones), making changes, are all like that analogy. If you look at the world's best entrepreneurs and businesspeople, they have a strange habit of throwing 20 things on the wall, seeing which of them stick, sweeping up the crap that didn't, and running like Hades with the things that worked.

The good news is that you can be smarter than that. While you know there are back roads to a better future in your practice, you can take the "highway" and the decision to remove most of the experimentation process. Reading this book was a first step in that direction; working with someone outside your office would be a second one; and obtaining additional processes already tidied up from all that wall staining would be even better.

It takes time and effort to get any new capability or expertise that you desire into place. If you wait until you're perfect at a new capability, you are unlikely to get very few of the right changes happening in your practice, or progress will go so slow that the positive effect you want will be as difficult to find as an honest pickpocket. Based on where you live, usually there is some sort of animal that winds up as "road kill" because it's too slow. Don't be road kill.

Let's face it: There are a lot of areas of your business that need your attention. I found that focusing my attention on what I'm best at and working with people who are good at what I'm not (and especially at the parts I don't like…) give me the best results. One of the secrets to my growth has been investing in myself through mentors. Each time I've done that, within a few months my investment has been paid back by clients who have then invested in themselves through me.

It doesn't matter how skilled you are if you don't have clients to work with. Your natural talent and your expertise have no impact if you are not getting to share your wealth with them, and thus receive the wealth that people have to share with you.

HOW CAN YOU EXPECT PEOPLE TO BE WILLING TO INVEST IN YOU IF YOU ARE NOT WILLING TO INVEST IN YOURSELF?

Another secret to my "Sales Mojo" has been the power of taking decisive action. I decided each time to invest in myself. And then others decided to invest in themselves through me. That is not just a coincidence.

That said, we covered a lot of different strategies and looked at some real-life example of what works. Let's take a few minutes to have a look at actual tools that you should be thinking about.

CHAPTER 17

Working, With or Without Technologies

"Winning isn't everything.
The will to prepare to win is everything."
Vince Lombardi

YOU NEED TO WORK TO WIN

If you are like me, you have heard the other statement given as a quote. You know the one: "Winning isn't everything, it is the only thing."

Well, guess what? that isn't what was said. Funny how the wrong quote can easily get perpetuated. Probably one of the most famously wrong quotes is "The coldest winter I ever spent was summer in San Francisco," widely misattributed to Mark Twain with the original origin unknown.

Unlike Twain's misquote which all are likely to find amusing, Lombardi's misquote results in a much bigger loss of meaning. (By the way, "winning" for this discussion is simply achieving some goal or being satisfied with an outcome that was desired.)

And if you thought that I would not address this topic in this book, well, you were wrong.

How many architects, business owners and people you know prepare ENOUGH to win, are willing to prepare to win, and especially are willing to prepare enough to ENSURE winning. Not a lot, right? Why is that? Because preparing takes work, time, and energy.

Most also refuse to seek out and invest in systems. SYSTEM is an acronym for Save-Your-Self-Time-Energy-Money. My guess is that the "will to prepare" got dropped from the quote because that implied work, and most don't relish the thought of doing work, especially if they don't like what they work at.

Speaking of "work," here's a diversion related to work and this concept of winning. Unless you were living under a rock for most of 2006-07, you probably witnessed a cultural phenomenon that swept much of the U.S., Canada and Australia called *The Secret.*

Essentially, the book and movie were about winning at life goals. One thing they were right on target about was making sure your head is screwed on correctly when it comes to the concept of how you think about money.

However, one minor (okay MAJOR) detail left out of "The Secret" was that WORK is actually involved to make desired results happen. Visualization and positive thinking can and do help smooth out the glide slope of the jet plane to success, but more often than not, work is involved all along the way to get to the landing strip.

By the way, let's also define that "work" often means effective delegation, as none of us can "do it all." Thus to accomplish the most, you must use effective delegation and the tools of accountability for what you delegate. Not only does it take time, energy, and work (or at least the work of delegation), but it takes knowing the right things to do or seeking help to find out the right things to do.

It is these "knowing" factors that make huge differences in our rates of success. In fact, you may likely do no more work than you would already have done. The difference is that you simply know what's more important to be doing and can skip the unimportant things. I'm sure you have done this in the past: erased a big chunk of work and had to do it a second time. And the second time was much faster since you knew what needed to be done.

Here's another way to understand how powerful this concept of "knowing" really is. You're probably familiar with the phrase "if I only knew what I know today when I was…."

HOW MANY TIMES HAS EACH OF US SAID THAT ONE?

About 10 years ago, I was saying, "If I only knew what I know today when I first got out of architectural school"; now I've regressed to, "If I only knew what I know today before I started college." Give me another five years and it'll be: "If I only knew what I know today when I exited the womb."

You get the point. Instead of the above, what if we looked at the ways to speed up knowing? Why not routinely ask, "What can I quickly do and 'know' that can bring me 10, 20, maybe even 30 years of knowing WITHOUT requiring 10-30 years of physical time?" That's a written goal of mine. I see that kind of process as the ultimate way to stop wasting time solving mysteries that someone else already spent valuable, nonrefundable time and effort solving.

By the way, many architects I interact with outside the Elite Architect Programs are unwilling to do much of any preparation or even supervise/delegate someone else to ensure winning, much less understand the value in "knowing." You probably have seen the same.

These architects' preparation for failure shows itself in a lack of coordinated strategy or focus, lack of any weekly statistical reports, and a lack of interpreting what the reports mean.

Preparing is about planning to do whatever it takes to get the job done. It's about using information to sequence out the path to getting the job. Preparing also involves analyzing the future and what it will take to make it the one you really want.

It's worth repeating: Creating the targets or goals is a major part of preparing. Since the unknown can't be prepared for, why not go ahead and define it? Especially knowing that if you define it, you'll very likely achieve it.

Take a look at how you prepare for each year, month, week and day. Make a commitment to prepare better. It takes some doing, but once it happens many stresses of "what's next" go away.

Finally and very importantly, don't leave out the preparing of yourself, so that YOU can better assume the leadership needed for the most successful client interactions possible. The emotional ability to look a client in the eye with comfort, caring and confidence is the one thing that 99 percent of your peers run screaming from, or tried to master half-heartedly and gave up.

ARCHITECTURAL TECHNOLOGY

As architects, you are indoctrinated early in your career to believe that more training with more titles equals more clients, and that the "better" your work is, the more people will know about your work and therefore the more projects you will get. I dissected those fallacies early on. In addition to this wrong thinking, you were also indoctrinated with the idea that modern technology, new programs, and technical gadgets are also significant contributors to having new clients go forward with new projects in your office.

Mr. Jack Canfield, author of the *New York Times* best seller *Chicken Soup for the Soul,* said something about success that really hit the nail on the head.

"Everything you want is just outside your comfort zone."

Robert Allen, author of

"The One Minute Millionaire: The Enlightened Way to Wealth"

You can play safe and spend $1,000 on the latest edition of AutoCAD and stay in your comfort zone. I guarantee you that this expense will not set you apart.

When I ask, "What is your biggest strength?" two out of three of my new members answer, "My team and I produce a solid set of drawings." I ask them, "Really, as opposed to what?" The reality is that this is exactly what everyone is saying to their prospects.

In this new architectural economy, your prospects will take it as a given that you can and will produce the documents of the highest quality for them and that you are using the latest technologies in your firm. After all, you are a registered architect and therefore should be able to produce good documents.

IF YOU'RE NOT, YOU'RE IN BIG TROUBLE.

Out in the practice world, we are inundated with materials and technology. Architects are very prone to signing up for the latest gadget, no matter how costly, because of this previous indoctrination that "technology sells architecture."

Let's face it. Most devices and any new software in your offices don't create a dollar of revenue on their own, or magically make a single client appear for a project, regardless of manufacturer claims. A harsh truth is that any technology or instrumentation that is beyond what is minimally necessary to accomplish a given task in a clinically acceptable manner is nothing more than a optional accessory.

One would hope that accessory at least made your practice easier, faster, or less complicated. Speed is the most often-cited reason a piece of technology belongs in your office, at least from the sales rep's and the manufacturer's perspective.

For practices seeking a constant flow of projects in this new architectural economy, by now you know that *you must market all the time.* Investing in new pieces of equipment and software can be the kiss of death for new project generation, by starving your marketing needs. Think about it: Not only do you have to pay for that new software, you also have to spend money on time to learn and be efficient with it before you can actually save any money with time.

Should you invest in new technology to stay in the Category of No. 1? Absolutely, but you first need to invest in a constant flow of new clients. Again, it's your new clients with their projects who will pay for your new technology, not the other way around.

That's it! I wish I could tell you that by investing in the latest software and other technologies, clients would fall in love with those things and decide to do millions worth of construction with you. But alas that isn't going to happen. Fortunately though, you don't need those things to make these projects happen.

It is in the best economical interests of those big companies that sell software to make you think that your career depends on whether you have that program.

MARKETING TECHNOLOGIES

Funny that I would include architectural and marketing technology in the same chapter, eh? Well, the reality is the marketing technology is just as important, or even more important.

While most of the profession worries about what the next program is (did someone said BIM?), and the need to run out and borrow money to buy and find time to learn and become efficient at it, the more important technologies you all need to be concerned about are the ones that leverage your marketing, make marketing easier, and improve your results at getting new clients with new projects.

If on Monday morning every architect would decide to spend half their technology time on this, more architecture would get done because the messages about architectural solutions would reach more of the population, and more clients would be helped. Unfortunately, that isn't going to happen, but by reading this you are more likely to do the things they aren't willing to do.

It seems that every time I send an e-mail about this topic I get a few e-mails from architects outraged that I can say things like this. They tell me that because of such powerful programs as BIM, they can produce documents four times faster and of much higher quality than any other firm. And for some strange reason, it seems that when I look at the website of those who are screaming, it is always a small firm, without any real project on display.

If you use marketing technologies effectively, they allow even the smallest office and solo architect to get big results. That's the true power of being smart about technology and casting your marketing net far and wide.

Here is a laundry list of current technologies that are playing a role or are on the leading edge of playing a role in helping get projects into the practice:

- Using automated response methods with mass media to handle and sort incoming calls (all on auto-pilot) so that half the battle has already been won.
- External and internal systems that automatically allow clients to self-select themselves so that you and your team only talk to on the phone or personally meet and present project to clients who are ready.
- Automatic and sequential follow-up systems so that clients enter your practice when they are ready.
- Using database profile services to look at your prospect database and see what the target client looks like for direct mail and niche marketing.
- Micro-niche direct mail (you have to use this one!)

- Website systems that force visitors into giving you their names and e-mail information to allow you to market to them over the long term.

- Using sequential auto-responders. (The best part of this one is that most people just don't get it that it is not you who just sent that e-mail.)

- Multiple media always at work and referring to one another. (This means printed, e-mail, recordings, etc., all working together in tandem to increase the total number of projects that go to construction.)

- Constant drip marketing that builds pools of target clients needing your help.

- Using Internet press releases for FREE media exposure; they make you an expert in your local market on any architectural topic you wish.

- Online video messages at your website, for use with AdWords, and via YouTube, etc., that give the right message and continue to make you the local "expert."

- Funneling correct secondary local domains into your website to boost traffic.

Many of these technologies have only existed for 12 months! That's how quickly marketing technology moves. It's not your fault you can't keep up with it. That's why there are experts to help architects make the most of all of this.

KEEPING THE TEAM MOTIVATED IN STRANGE TIMES

On the recession front, there's no doubt that what was economically local and restricted to some locations has now spread to most markets. Regardless of how slow or non-existent economic growth is in any region, consumers are at the very least concerned and may be panicked.

On a brighter note, there are ways to stay profitable in any type of economy. As business owners, it's a prerequisite that you have a different mindset: Put all the things you see and hear via the news, and over which you have no control, into a box and set it to the side. Get it out of your field of vision.

Acknowledge that those things exist, then pay attention to what you can influence – including tangible things like marketing, purchases and investment decisions in the business, sales process, setting timelines for equipment upgrades, matching staff to work flow, etc.

Our teams have a harder time with the "boxing" of what's happening outside the practice. Even the most ardent entrepreneurial-oriented team member can find his or her spirit dampened by recent events. As part of your effort to insulate your workforce, this is a reminder to always take some time to inject more team grit into the office and to remind your staff that, as a team, you know how to be successful. Here are some strategies you can use with your team to help you stay on top of your game, or roll with the punches, whatever your circumstances may be.

1) FOSTER GRATITUDE FOR WHAT EVERYONE HAS.

Focusing with gratitude on all the things we do have, rather than what we don't, immediately puts us into an appreciative frame of mind. Gratitude is an incredible antidote to fear: It expands our perspective and makes us concentrate on the big picture, since the very things we're grateful for are often things that others lack.

Fear, however, does just the opposite: It contracts our thinking, shrinks our perspective, and keeps us isolated from taking action.

2) STAY FOCUSED ON THE POSITIVE.

Our level of confidence has a lot to do with our ability to take action and move things ahead. Starting your staff meetings and morning huddles with the requirement that each team member discuss what was positive in the last week/day (business or personal) helps the staff realize that good things are happening and that, as a team, you're making progress. This helps with team confidence.

If you haven't done this exercise before, the way to start is to explain it, then say, "Since we haven't done this before, would everyone be willing for me to go first?" After you discuss what was positive for you in the last day/week, others will fall right into line.

3) FOCUS ON WHAT IS WORKING VERSUS WHAT'S NOT.

Even in the worst situations, something is still working. Sit down with your team (or office manager) and think through one of your current challenges, focusing on what's working versus what's not. This is a way to remind us that we always have a choice about how we respond to negative situations - either reactively or creatively.

Reactive responses often involve blame, guilt, anger, depression, even addictions or violence. The alternative is to choose a creative response such as discussing things through with your closest advisers, meditation, prayer, or exercising to burn off excess energy.

You'll notice that "reactive" and "creative" contain the same letters but rearranged, just as you can do with your perspective. What you need to keep in mind is that focusing on what's working puts you back into a creative mode so you can come up with strategies for fixing what's not.

Afterword

"Tell me and I'll forget, show me and I may remember, involve me and I'll understand."
Tanja Siebert

Congratulations! If you've followed this system and done most things reasonably right, a larger amount of the project presentations you do will go forward with construction. You can sequence the project and look forward to putting your architectural skills to work helping the clients contacting your office, and you now have access to clients that none of your peers will be competing for.

Was it a lot of work? Damn straight! Was all that effort worth it? Well, only if you think that working on projects with the fees you deserve is worth doing.

And only if you want to help more clients who really need the best that architecture and you can offer. When you think about it in those terms, architects working on the projects for the clients they want and members of the Elite Architect Programs all shout with a loud "YES!"

The systems and marketing that allow this to happen are more than worth it.

A WORD ABOUT GEOGRAPHY

The principles discussed in this book work whether you are in London, UK; London, Ontario; or New London, Connecticut. They work whether you're in Paris, France, or Paris, Texas; or Sydney, Australia, or Sydney, North Dakota.

Yes, the local dialect needs to be tweaked in the materials (or even translated), but the principles of direct response work everywhere. That's why members in the Elite Architect Programs get similar results wherever they are in the world. Clients with a potential project want the same thing from people in our field no matter where they live on the planet. *Finally – something that's the same everywhere!*

All we need are mass-media mechanisms and the right message to broadcast into the marketplace. Architects, like most business owners, want to say, "But my business is different" – or, in this case, "My country is different."

The reality is that problem-solution based marketing works great anywhere in the world when it is deployed to help architectural clients. Architectural boards, colleges, and rule-makers are different worldwide, but there is an uncanny similarity in the rules they make up that architects must abide by.

We fulfill the letter of the law with our marketing but limit ourselves no further in any way beyond what the specific law of a state or province requires.

ELITE ARCHITECTS PROGRAMS AVAILABLE TO YOU

This select group of architects is part of my intensive *Elite Architect Programs*, where all our advertisements, project acceptance systems and marketing strategies are taught to them to use in their practices. Unfortunately, the program can only accept a certain number of architects each year, since I am in contact with each one and there is only so much time in a week. Therefore, I restrict the number of members I accept for the different programs.

I've always been a big proponent of the 80/20 rule, which says you can waste your time on the 80 percent who will generate nothing or you can focus your attention and time on the 20 percent who will generate everything. It's your decision. This book has shown you the best path for you to achieve your goals. It is different from the path most of your peers take, and that's a good thing.

FOR MORE INFORMATION, VISIT

www.ArchitectProfits.com

TO HAVE MORE STORIES LIKE THESE IN YOUR PRACTICE, FOLLOW THE PRINCIPLES IN THIS BOOK!

"The topics we covered and the information and advice Christian gave me during my first one-on-one phone call have really made a massive impact to what I am doing now and to how I am going to go forward into the future. I'm in the process of making sweeping changes to my website and my practice strategies and I can't wait to see the positive differences I know they'll make."

Daniel Sandbrook
LeHouse Architecture, Australia

"I have spent many years learning how to promote my firm, from different seminars, books and other paid professionals. I can say without a doubt that Christian is providing extremely valuable information and that he is right on target with his Architect Marketing System. I would recommend the Elite Architects Programs to any Architect, especially for those taking their first step toward marketing themselves."

Ron Cosentino
Cosentino Architecture, PLLC, New York

"I have been reading many books and have been to many seminars on marketing and none of them have clicked with me as to how they would work for selling design services. Your information and strategies on how to promote services have been making perfect sense to me. Many of these are the reasons I decided to start my own practice."

James D. Kavanagh, AIA
studio591 architecture, llc, Pottstown, PA

"I've been looking for ways to market and promote my practice for a long time. As you know, there just isn't much out there just for us Architects when comes to marketing or creating a better sales process that reduces fee issues.

I came across Christian Hogue's Architecture Marketing System surfing the Internet, and to be honest I was pretty skeptical. I had never heard of anyone in our field making these kind of claims at being willing to show me the hidden secrets to finding more clients for my practice, much less someone who's been practicing himself (one of us)! So, even though I was skeptical, I decided to "test-drive" the Elite Architects Program as I was looking to find new ways to add new clients into my firm. I figured, why not, as it's guaranteed and free for the first two months.

Results? Well, I used just one strategy from Christian's system which got me my first client who is going forward with a retainer, all within the first two months of 'test-driving' the strategies explained in the AMS! The best part is that it cost me *less than $150 to get this new client by using this strategy!!! This one project will result in a fee of roughly 75k (no need to say that I am using this strategy again as I'm writing this...) which means a 30:1 return of investment for an entire year of the highest level of Christian's program with only one project!*

There's a point where we all wish we could have done certain things over, so here's my opinion for anyone who wants to avoid having any regrets in the area of marketing and promotion for their architecture practice. If you are a firm owner that is serious about your work and are willing to take action, get more projects using ways that the majority in the profession will never seek to understand, and finally know how to target the clients you want (no matter what the economy is doing), you would be a fool not to join his Elite Program."

Orlando Lamas
Principal, Fortis Lamas Associates, FL

"I have been in the industry for almost 35 years and been through countless courses and seminars searching for key methods to market my firm. After finding out information about Christian's program and learning from his material, I've decided that I could've really used this information 30 years ago! Right away after our first one on one phone call, I was 100% convinced that Christian's strategies and input would improve my business.

I would recommend for other Architects to take part in the Elite Architect Program, whether they are new to marketing strate-

gies or not. I am so happy to have found this program. It is exactly what I've been searching for to help promote my services from start to finish, and provide me with clever step by step tips to reach the results I want with my clients… especially in these difficult times."

Jack Johnston
Golden Rule Remodeling & Architecture , Salem, OR

"Dear Christian, just to let you know, Chris had a very positive meeting with our clients yesterday and it looks as though the project will be going ahead over the next couple of weeks!!! We are very excited about this new important project. Also, we have had very positive responses from the Real Estate Agents: "superb and professional presentation." We now move forward with great confidence because of what we have learned in such a short time from your program!

To be honest, we were very skeptical that what works in the U.S. would work here in New Zealand. Based on our results, I'd be very surprised if your system didn't work wherever the local architect is in the world. U.S. and International Architects should be lining up for what Christian has so graciously made available to the profession. Thank you again for how you have helped us during this first month and especially the insights Chris has been given from your material – from an architect's perspective."

Robyn MacPherson
MacPherson Architecture, New Zealand

There are simple actions to be taken

while the rest of the field remains paralyzed

or stuck in the "good old days."

Reading this book was one of them;

now you need to act on at least three

of the most inspiring strategies

you have learned in this book.

If you can't think of three right now,

you need to read this book again and

pay more attention to what you are reading.

That's an easy action you can take right now.

Get to it!

Advantage Media Group is proud to be a part of the Tree Neutral™ program. Tree Neutral offsets the number of trees consumed in the production and printing of this book by taking proactive steps such as planting trees in direct proportion to the number of trees used to print books. To learn more about Tree Neutral, please visit **www.treeneutral.com**. To learn more about Advantage Media Group's commitment to being a responsible steward of the environment, please visit **www.advantagefamily.com/green**

THE PROFITABLE ARCHITECT is available in bulk quantities at special discounts for corporate, institutional, and educational purposes. To learn more about the special programs Advantage Media Group offers, please visit **www.KaizenUniversity.com** or call 1.866.775.1696.

THE MOST INCREDIBLE FREE GIFT JUST FOR YOU!!!

Did you really think I was going to let you go on your own without offering you a great gift to ensure that you will get the most out of what you read in this book? Of course not!

Now that you've learned a great deal, gained great strategies, and you have tools and a specific step-by-step system to put in place, it's time for me to make sure that you start working with these tools the right way in your own practice. But how?

Very simple: I want to give you the opportunity to benefit from 20 min of my time FOR FREE, to talk together about what first steps you need to put in place in your own practice and what you will need to fix first to get the results you want as quickly as possible.

You just need to send me a short e-mail to schedule your complimentary session with me at:

TheProfitableArchitect@ArchitectProfits.com

P.S.: As you might know from visiting my website (www.ArchitectProfits.com), people pay up to $679 just to talk with me about their website. As you can imagine, I do get a lot of requests for these free sessions. Therefore, I have a specific number of spots available each month, so be sure to **schedule your spot right away!**

www.ingramcontent.com/pod-product-compliance
Lightning Source LLC
LaVergne TN
LVHW050615100826
845148LV00011B/1600

* 9 7 8 1 5 9 9 3 2 2 0 0 1 *